HAUNTED DALTON, GEORGIA

HAUNTED DALTON, GEORGIA

CONNIE HALL-SCOTT

Haunted America

Published by Haunted America
A Division of The History Press
Charleston, SC 29403
www.historypress.net

First published 2013

Manufactured in the United States

ISBN 978.1.60949.789.7

Library of Congress CIP data applied for.

Notice: The information in this book is true and complete to the best of our knowledge. It is offered without guarantee on the part of the author or The History Press. The author and The History Press disclaim all liability in connection with the use of this book.

CONTENTS

Preface

Fear is a powerful emotion, and fear of the unknown is perhaps the most primal of all. Everyone is familiar with it, from the time we are infants protesting the dark to when we grow older and actually choose to be confronted with things that terrorize us, albeit normally from the safety of a theater seat or through the pages of a book we can put down when the reading gets too uncomfortable.

Since ancient times, people have enjoyed the thrill that accompanies the sudden shock of being scared and the adrenaline rush experienced when we're afraid. Ghost stories, particularly those seeped in history, enable us to indulge the bizarre pleasure derived from entertaining our fears.

That's why you're holding this book right now, isn't it?

Ghosts—souls of the dead that, for whatever reason, remain earthbound—are mysterious. They represent the unknown. For those who are able to think outside the box long enough to consider the very real possibility that they can and do exist, ghosts are sources of both intrigue and fear.

I started life as an unlikely candidate to write a book about ghosts. I was the child lying in bed at night with the covers pulled up to my chin in a large house on a hill too far removed from civilization for my comfort. Each night, I waited, half paralyzed, for the pale boy I had seen on *Salem's Lot* to tap on my bedroom window requesting an invitation to come inside. Up into my twenties I slept with a nightlight on, just in case he finally found me.

Actively exploring the unknown began for me when Leona Blevins, editor of the *Whitfield-Murray Advertiser*, asked me to write a couple of local haunt stories in the late '90s in recognition of Halloween. The result was a miniature glimpse into both Dalton and Tunnel Hill's legends and lore. I had fun with it, I learned a lot and I realized people—folks in my own backyard—have dealt with, or are dealing with, things I had conveniently managed to convince myself weren't real.

Shortly after the turn of the century, I fell in love with one of Dalton's best-known haunted locations when my father purchased, restored and reopened the historic Wink Theatre. I worked there for a while and listened to numerous area residents tell of their own past experiences at the Wink. I was quickly surprised by how many stories of first kisses and near misses were accompanied by sincere accounts of ghostly encounters.

I often led tours through the Wink, telling this group or that about how the theater was the first air-conditioned building in downtown Dalton and how it is among the last remaining examples of art moderne architecture in the South, and so on. To spice things up a bit, I began throwing in the occasional story about the "lady in the restroom" or the "giggling ghost children." It was those stories and my listeners' genuine interest that led to the formation of Dalton Ghost Tours.

I created Dalton Ghost Tours in 2003 in an effort to share the city's wealth of ghostly goings-on. As I began to research other historic locations with alleged spectral attachments, I was amazed by how easy it was to uncover local haunts. Perhaps I shouldn't have been too surprised, considering the richness of history, personalities and culture present in Dalton.

Over the last decade, I've been asked to speak on the topic of Dalton's haunted happenings at various civic organizations, social clubs and schools; on television and radio; and for a couple of films. I was invited to teach a class on local legend at Dalton State College's Continuing Education Center in 2009. Because of the class's popularity, I would go on to teach Ghostbusting 101 and Ghostbusting 102 on the Dalton State campus to full-capacity classrooms.

The primordial desire to be frightened abounds, and there are enough things that go bump in the night in northwest Georgia to go around. I'm always happy to share what I have learned.

I hope this book will help you face some of your own fears. You know, those things you're afraid of but don't want to admit aloud—things such as haunted houses, menacing dolls, dark cemeteries, abandoned ghost-filled buildings and that hand you're sure will reach up and pull you under if you let your arm or foot dangle off the edge of your bed too long. Hey, I'm not judging. I'm here to help. By vicariously facing your fears with this book, you might be able to tame them or, at least, convince yourself that you have. That is, until the next time the icy fingers of terror squeeze your heart and you hear the voice of the unknown whisper your name from the darkest corner of your own shadow-filled bedroom.

ACKNOWLEDGEMENTS

This book is dedicated to my mamaw, Frances Evelyn Bryant-Fowler, who always believed in me and who taught me the love of storytelling from her front porch swing, and to my papaw, Sam Henry Fowler.

I would like to thank the following people for their vast and unique contributions to this book.

First, thank you, Amy Petulla, author of *Haunted Chattanooga* and proprietor of Chattanooga Ghost Tours, for introducing me to the creative team that is The History Press. Thanks also to everyone who shared stories with me over the years. All of you helped bring this project to life.

Huge thanks go to my awesome photographers Robert Hartline and Angela Moss and to those who loaned photos from their private collections.

I extend mega appreciation to the Hurst family, Marcelle White and the Whitfield-Murray Historical Society, my friends at the *Daily Citizen-News*, Ken Sumner, the Tunnel Hill Historical Foundation, Lea Hartline, the late Kenneth and Barbara Holcomb and the late Dr. L.E. Patterson. I wish to thank Randy Bates, Katie Soesbee and Leslie Waycaster for indulging my questions on their beautiful buildings. Also, I am grateful to David Hamilton, who quit this earth way too soon, for his friendship and mentorship.

For sharing insight into the world that lurks beneath the veil, I thank Victoria Bragg, Reece Christian and last, but never least, Drew Hester, with whom I've shared a lot of strange happenings, from the Bell Witch to chills in Chickamauga and beyond.

Thanks to my personal proofreaders and soundboards: Juanita Hall, my very cherished and very giving mama; Samantha Hall-Turner, she who is most genetically like me in all the world; and Angela Hall-Smith, my "number one fan" and sister-friend. Thank you, too, to Troy Hall, my daddy, for your love and for all that you do for us, including, but not limited to, buying me that fabulous red Corvette that I never properly thanked you for because once upon a time I might have been a brat. Thanks also to my sweet aunt Phyllis Bradley and my BFFs Christi Michael-Screws, Ron Chastain and Lynn Hutchison. I love each of you to the moon.

The biggest thanks of all go out to the holders of my heart, my true loves—Adam, Aaron and Lexi Scott, who are my greatest contribution to life—and to God without whom nothing would be possible.

INTRODUCTION

Whether or not you believe in ghosts, know this: everything you are about to read is real. At least it's real to those who were brave enough to share their strange stories and to those who did their part in paying homage to the time-honored tradition of handing down the same terrific tales that were told to them. In addition to sharing those accounts with you, I have logged untold hours prowling through old newspapers and records, reading history books, conversing with area historians and exploring the haunt-filled locations you will read about.

Nestled in the foothills of the spectacular North Georgia mountains, Dalton is perhaps best known as the Carpet Capital of the World, producing 90 percent of the United States' carpet. It is also a thriving tourist town, offering unique shopping opportunities, mouthwatering local cuisine, performing arts, exceptional architecture and an abundance of historic destinations with Civil War, Native American and railroad highlights. Able to boast world-celebrated trails for mountain biking and hiking, breathtaking rivers and lakes for fishing and boating, opportunities for golf and tennis and so much more, Whitfield County is a virtual haven for lovers of the outdoors. Filled with both transients and plenty of folks with deep roots, Dalton is rich in personality and diversity.

All these things sound great—and they are—but every coin is two sided. For every beautiful old home that reminds us of the city's southern culture and charm, there's another seeped in shadowy mystery. As we celebrate Whitfield County's history through Civil War reenactments in Tunnel Hill, the annual Prater's Mill Country Fair in Cohutta, the Liberty Tree Festival in downtown Dalton and other fun-filled community events, we sometimes forget the nightmarish scars left on the skin of North Georgia by a horrific war that took place over 150 years ago and, before that, the suffering of the Cherokees who were driven from their "Enchanted Land" in an atrocity remembered as the Trail of Tears. All too often, tragedies such as these are recipes for troubled spirits unwilling to move on to what awaits them beyond this life. Add to those monumental events the inevitable instances of murder, mayhem and madness, and it is no wonder so many people report ghastly—or rather, ghostly—activity.

I invite you to come with me on a journey that will take you deep inside Dalton's hair-raising legends and supernatural happenings. Together, we'll take a peek beneath life's shadowy veil to examine some of the things we were told didn't exist when we were children.

Through the pages that follow, I'll lead you down the aisles and behind the scenes of one of the South's most haunted historic theaters, inside which the restless spirit of a mystery woman reaches out to guests, ghost children laugh and play and poltergeist activity abounds. I'll introduce you to the weeping girl, who believed she couldn't live another day without the man she loved so she elected not to and is now held captive within the walls of the former Hotel Dalton by her own fear. We'll retrace the final steps of a murderer who was hanged, drop in on the tormented soul of a lynched man and step inside haunted houses. You'll meet a long-dead fireman who gets a kick out of playing tricks on the living. Take my hand as we tiptoe through cemeteries where some of the dead refuse to rest. Hold on tight while we explore war-tainted fields and woods so riddled with rowdy spirits that grown men have refused to return.

Oh, the places you'll go!

I'm going to educate you with history, entertain you with lore and keep you up at night. So, are you ready?

CHAPTER ONE

THE VERY HAUNTED HISTORIC WINK THEATRE

I don't believe in ghosts, but I'm afraid of them.
Mark Twain

J.C.H. Wink had a dream. He wanted to create a place for the citizens of Dalton to meet up and relax and enjoy popcorn and a soda while watching a movie, a place that would transport patrons away from the worries and tragedies of World War II, if only for a few hours. He dreamed of creating a small-town version of Atlanta's Fox Theatre.

Construction began on the Wink Theatre in 1939 on the ground where the Shadowland Theater, a silent film house, had stood for many years. Gertrude McFarland, born in 1926, remembers walking around downtown Dalton when she was a child and stopping in the entrance of the Shadowland, by this time already closed. "I would press my nose up so I could see in the distance the seats and I could imagine what it was like when it had been a theater," she once told me.

The doors of the Wink opened to the public for the first time on a Monday night, September 7, 1941. Excited patrons flocked to the town's first air-conditioned building with 1,550 luxurious body-contoured chairs and the most up-to-date sound system available to see Joan Crawford and Melvyn Douglas light up the silver screen in *They All Kissed the Bride*. Tickets were eleven and thirty cents.

Opening night was a success, but sadly, J.C.H. Wink was not in attendance. Or, perhaps he was. Later, some would wonder if he had not, quite literally,

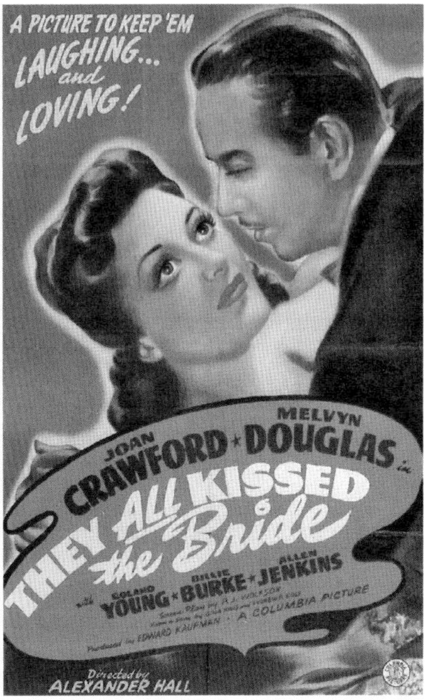

They All Kissed the Bride was the first movie shown at the Wink in 1941. *Photo courtesy of Columbia Pictures.*

been there in spirit. Mr. Wink passed away before the theater was complete, but generations of Whitfield County residents would grow up enjoying the fruits of his dream.

"The Wink Theatre was the fabric of your entire life if you grew up in Dalton," Flora Caldwell once told *Daily Citizen-News* reporter Nancy Carney.

"They built the Wink when I was in high school," Gertrude McFarland shared with me. "We had our baccalaureate ceremony at the Wink. Dalton High School, class of 1943. I graduated right during the war. Half of my class went on to World War II and didn't come back."

Attorney Randy Bates told Scotti O'Neill of the *Daily Citizen-News* in February 1990 that "the Wink is the place where most of us either received our first kiss or first slap; it's more than just brick and mortar."

News editor of the *Daily Citizen* Wes Chance remembers spending Saturday afternoons at the "kiddie" matinee feasting on Jerry Lewis and Elvis Presley movies, getting to buy a pickle for a nickel and once watching a live stage show staring Bob Brandy and hoping he'd be picked to sit on Brandy's horse, Rebel.

Wes also remembers a stern-looking woman to whom nobody dared give backtalk. She manned the concession stand in the mid- to late '60s. Sometimes accompanying her was "the man who never spoke," Wes wrote in a column published in the '90s. The man was mute, and his job was to tear tickets and police the theater with his dreaded flashlight, making sure all feet were on the floor.

I too have memories of the Wink. In the '70s, my mother often took my sister and me to see Disney classics, such as *The Rescuers*, *Escape to Witch Mountain* and *Bambi*. Once, I watched a scary movie about killer worms with my mom and dad and their ever-present friends Ronnie and Brenda Houston. As a couple of fishermen in a rowboat conversed on screen and I waited in terror for their fishing worms to escape and devour them, a plastic toy bracelet I had gotten earlier in the day snapped apart and pinched my six-year-old wrist. Certain the worms had somehow made their way off the screen and onto my arm, I began screaming and struggling to escape our aisle.

A patron of the Wink in the 1950s. This photo was shared with me shortly after the Wink reopened in 2002. *Collection of Connie Hall-Scott.*

"It wasn't even during a scary part," Mom later laughed, recalling my hysterics that made those seated around us either laugh or frown.

I also remember going upstairs to the bathroom. Unnecessary bathroom visits are a rite of passage for most youngsters. Trips to the Wink bathroom stand out in my mind as somehow both frightening and alluring. As kids seem to be more able to do, I sensed something a little, well, "off"—something ethereal. Later, I would learn that I wasn't the only one to experience that "not alone" sensation in the ladies' room.

And I remember the ornate gates leading up to the third floor that were always locked because the balcony was closed to the public sometime in the '70s. I used to stand in front of the gate with my hands gripping the bars and my face pressed against it as I marveled what was in the darkness on the other side. I'd still like to know.

Due to urban sprawl and the opening of more modern theaters outside downtown Dalton, the Wink closed in 1981 with a final showing of Disney's *The Black Hole*. Ironic, considering that's what the theater would become—a virtual black hole—over the next decades as it rotted and decayed before an unsophisticated audience of pigeons and rats.

A Dalton Ghost Tour guest once recalled "dragging Main Street" in front of the Wink in the '80s. Before the city banned the activity, masses of teens commonly cruised and parked along the streets of historic downtown Dalton to socialize.

"I was talking to a group of friends," the tour guest shared. "Suddenly one of them jumped back and yelled. The dude said he saw a woman looking out one of the windows up above the marquee. The theater was dark and deserted. Nobody could have been in there, but I saw her. Only for a moment before she faded."

There are two windows above the marquee, both belonging to the projection room. Several young people saw the woman looking out one of those windows that afternoon, the eyewitness told me, goose bumps lighting up his arms. He claimed he didn't believe in ghosts until that day but that he is now an unashamed believer.

Leon Hurst didn't believe in ghosts either, until he moved his family to Dalton and took over management of the Wink in 1972. I had the pleasure of chatting with Mr. and Mrs. Hurst, their son Dale and his wife, Dana, a couple years ago about the theater's haunted happenings.

"I have no doubt it is haunted," Leon told me during our talk as he and his family shared the unexplainable experiences they encountered up until the time the theater shut down.

Leon's office was located between the ladies' and the men's restrooms on the second floor. He told me about hearing children laughing and playing outside his door, often when the theater was closed for the evening and he was alone inside. Sometimes, he heard bells jingling in conjunction with the laughter. He described the bells as "like the ones parents used to attach to their young children's shoes to keep up with them." Upon opening his office door after hearing those sounds, Leon would always find the area empty.

Leon recalled seeing his office doorknob turn with no one on the other side to turn it. Sometimes the knob turning would be followed by an impression left in the leather seat across from his desk. He wondered if J.C.H. Wink might have come back to check on him, to make sure he was doing a good job managing the theater.

Acting as projectionist, Dale Hurst has witnessed film shoot off reels spontaneously. He would go on to work for Carmike Cinemas for a number of years, managing the theater at Walnut Square Mall before taking a job with Carmike Corporate, but can think of no logical explanation for film flying off reels. It has only happened to him within the walls of the Wink. He has also heard a host of strange noises and has felt an unseen presence on more than one occasion.

Leon Hurst told Neely Young, the former publisher of the *Daily Citizen-News*, about some of his spooky experiences in an article titled "Child Lives at the Wink" that ran on April 16, 1980:

> *A strange thing occurred one Sunday afternoon at 12:30. No one was at the theater but me, and I began to hear a hammering sound. I went down into the auditorium, and it sounded like someone beating the walls with a hammer. I figured some construction was taking place next door. Upon checking, I found there was not a single person in any of the buildings in the entire block. The hammering continued for about 10 minutes and stopped. This happened for two consecutive Sunday afternoons and lasted about 10 minutes each time.*

Then there's the time Dale was sweeping up, pushing his broom down the left aisle toward the stage and listening to music on his boom box. Dale was alone in the theater, or so he believed. Suddenly, the volume of his music mysteriously decreased. He felt a chill and the familiar sense of an unseen presence. Determined not to give in to his mounting fear, Dale continued to sweep until he heard the distinct sound of "giant footsteps running down the aisle" toward him. He quickly turned, prepared to face whoever or whatever was there. Only, no one and nothing was. At least, not anyone or anything he could see with the naked eye. That's when the volume on his jam box increased to the maximum level. Dale put his broom down, walked out of the theater and locked up, not bothering to go around and turn the lights off.

The Wink auditorium, post renovation. Dale Hurst was pushing a broom down the left aisle in the '70s when he had a brush with the paranormal. *Photo by Connie Hall-Scott.*

"There is something there," Dale once told me. "Whether it's good, bad or indifferent, it's there. I have two college degrees. I consider myself to be pretty well educated and scientifically oriented. Just because something goes bump in the night doesn't mean I think it's a ghost, spirit or something like that. You've got to prove something to me."

When it comes to the Wink Theatre, Dale Hurst has received ample proof. His assessment is it's haunted.

As the theater sat dilapidating, worry began. No one wanted to see the lovely art moderne structure disappear. There was talk of leveling it and building a parking deck. Bruce and Gaile Jennings, Mary Gene Dykes, Randy Bates and others were among the first who made important efforts to see the theater brought back to life. Save the Wink committees and a task force were formed, and progress was made, but not enough. Nobody, it seemed, wanted to put forth the money—in excess of a million dollars—not to mention the massive amount of work and time, to breathe life back into the Wink.

I was just as surprised as anyone when my father, Troy Hall, decided to take the Wink on. He purchased it from the city for $100,001 in 1998 and began a restoration process that would take close to four years. He had his own memories of growing up with the Wink, watching westerns and hits such as *Gone with the Wind*, to propel his decision to take on the task. The doors reopened in 2002 with a sold-out performance of the *Platters*. Already, strange happenings were afoot.

Isidro Esparza, a handyman employed by my father, claimed he didn't believe in ghosts. He often found himself working in the theater, sometimes alone. "It was right before the grand reopening," Isidro told me. "I was sitting in the storage room on the second floor. I had been hammering some nails in a wall. I put the hammer down and grabbed my water bottle. The hammering started back up all on its own! Nobody was in there but me. I sat and listened, and I tried to figure it out. It kept going for several minutes, and I never figured it out."

Hammering, just like Leon Hurst had heard years before. When Isidro first told me of his experience, I wondered if he might have heard Leon's story somewhere and run with it. He hadn't. In fact, he hadn't lived in Georgia terribly long, certainly not in the '80s when Neely Young wrote of Mr. Hurst's eerie experiences.

My dad did a great job renovating the Wink Theatre, sparing no expense. I'm proud of the work he did there. Some of the unique finishing touches include a replica of the original ticket booth and renovation of the Wink

A view of the Wink staircase as it appeared in 1998 before renovation began. *Photo by Connie Hall-Scott.*

Left: My daughter, Lexi, on the post-renovation staircase inside the Wink. *Photo by Connie Hall-Scott.*

Below: The Wink today. *Photo by Robert Hartline.*

marquee, which features the original blinking "Wink" sign donated by the Wink family. Color schemes throughout the interior were matched to the original colors. Ornamental plasters, sculptures and friezes were delicately crafted by artist Wei Ning "Mouse" Song, a native of China. Over 1,100 seats, replicas of those in New York's Carnegie Hall, were placed in the auditorium and on the balcony, the only difference being the cast-iron panels found on Wink aisle seats. All possible original structures were preserved to assure the theater's placement on the National Register of Historic Places. The lighting and sound is state of the art. The reopening was an exciting time for Dalton.

For three years the newly reopened Wink served the community as a venue for the performing arts, a reception hall, a modern movie house and a place for social gatherings and cultural events.

It was after a showing of *Gone with the Wind*, shortly after the reopening, that Jennifer Ingraham Cline had a brush with the paranormal. Jennifer, along with her mother, Stephanie Ingraham, was an active volunteer prior to and after the reopening. Jennifer volunteered to rewind the film reel the day after the showing only to have the film shoot from the reels as other reels had done years before with Dale Hurst. Keep in mind that the projection equipment was brand-new and therefore not the same machine used back

Rehearsal for *The King & I*, as directed by Tony Smithy. It was the first play to be performed in the Wink following the reopening. Cast and crew reported hearing phantom footsteps coming from the empty rooms upstairs as well as having eerie feelings while in the dressing rooms. *Photo by Connie Hall-Scott.*

This lit-up marquee announced a play directed by me that took place following the Wink's reopening. During this production, several cast members reported strange happenings inside the theater. *Photo by Larry Hall.*

in the '70s when the Hurst family ran the theater. Also remember that self-ejecting film is not normal. If it's not normal, it's paranormal.

"This is typical poltergeist activity," my longtime friend and parapsychologist Drew Hester opined. "Basically this means that a spirit was able to obtain enough energy to literally take over the projection reels and control them itself. This doesn't mean it was doing it in a harmful way, but more than likely, it was just trying to make itself known. Most of the time when a ghost makes a noise or creates activity, it's doing so to gain attention."

For over a year, I worked at the theater as a director. Patrons would come in the ticket office to share stories of their Wink memories. I began hearing more and more about "the lady in the bathroom."

As mentioned earlier, when I was a little girl, I had an odd feeling when visiting the second floor. Turns out I wasn't the only one. I never saw anything, but I sure sensed something. Over the years, handfuls of people have brought up our ethereal lady in the Wink bathroom. Some claim

Parapsychologist Drew Hester at the Wink, in front of the set of double doors with a reputation for unlocking themselves. *Photo by Connie Hall-Scott.*

to have seen her, usually out of the corner of an eye. These days when speaking with a group embarking on a ghost tour with me, I talk about the Wink. Every so often, a hand will go up or someone will speak out and tell about the mysterious woman they crossed paths with before the Wink closed in 1981. Some women tell me they were children at the time and that the lady reached out to them before vanishing. Others report having felt a drop in temperature, or a cold spot, in her presence.

Who she is, is impossible to say. As far as I know, no one died on site. No one I've spoken with seems to know who she is or what she wants. This lady is most apt to make her spectral self known to other females. I've yet to hear from a male witness.

In the winter of 2003, Judy Hall, a cousin by marriage, ventured upstairs to the restroom during a concert. She believed herself alone. While in the first stall, she heard a flush coming from a neighboring stall.

"Hello?" she ventured. No one answered. After exiting her stall, she glanced under the door of the other stalls only to find none occupied. Knowing she had indeed heard a flush, she began pushing the doors open one by one. When she came to the last door, she opened it, and the toilet flushed before her eyes. Judy said she would never again go upstairs alone.

Custodians employed by my family claim the lady played occasional tricks on them. Stall doors opened and closed. Toilets flushed. Toilet seats that, moments before, were down were found raised, and vice versa.

Strange and unexplained stories about the Wink began circulating as early as the 1950s. A former employee during that time period once told me about how management used to leave after locking up, only to return the next day to find the far left set of a trio of double doors sometimes unlocked. The same thing happened in the 1970s, not often, but often enough. After the Wink reopened in 2002, it would happen again. I know, for sure, that the theater was always locked up after closing each

The ladies' bathroom on the second floor of the Wink. The door standing open shows the view observed by a patron who witnessed phantom flushing. Others have reported encountering a ghostly presence in and around this room. *Photo by Connie Hall-Scott.*

day or night. However, from time to time the doors on the far left would be unlocked the next morning.

I need to point out that the original six Wink doors were replaced with replicas. The doorframe was replaced as well. So, the problem isn't mechanical. And I can vouch that the error wasn't human either during the time my family operated the theater. None of us was willing to take a security risk on a costly investment by foolishly leaving doors unlocked. The only reasoning left when normal doesn't apply is paranormal.

The owner of Chastain Glass in Dalton ended up with the original Wink doors. The doors are now stored in the company's warehouse. Rhonda Chastain, employee and daughter of the owner, believes the doors came with a spirit attached.

"There are often noises in that area of the warehouse," Rhonda shared. "It sounds as if someone is slamming the [Wink] doors that are propped up against a wall. When we go check things out, everything's in place. Nothing has been moved. It's very strange."

Rhonda said it isn't uncommon to feel "creeped out" when in the area of the warehouse near the doors. She believes that whatever caused the unlocking of the doors while they were attached to the theater still has an attachment to the doors in both locations.

"They're haunted objects," she declared. "There's a story there that we'll probably never know."

I agree with Rhonda. I believe ghosts sometimes attach themselves to material possessions like important pieces of jewelry, a car they loved or even furniture. Clearly, whatever spirit has formed an attachment to the doors of the Wink Theatre has a significant connection with them. Attaching one's spirit self to a collection of doors is admittedly peculiar. I mean, if I were dead and kept going back to something from my life, I doubt it would be sets of doors. But for a moment, let's open our minds and imaginations.

Let us take a leap and try to imagine why a spirit would focus energies on unlocking and drawing attention to those doors. Maybe J.C.H. Wink or someone closely associated with the theater in life is merely trying to beckon patrons inside: "Come on in, enjoy!" Or it could be someone, like the doorman Wes Chance remembers, has yet to realize he doesn't have to work anymore and busies himself with former chores. Or perhaps, a particularly helpful or frustrated spirit wants someone, anyone, to come inside and help another seriously stuck earthbound spirit—such as the woman in the bathroom—move on. Or possibly, the door-focused spirit made a significant choice in life that involved either staying at or leaving the theater at some

Original Wink doors, pre-renovation. The doors now belong to the owner of Chastain Glass. Rhonda Chastain believes the doors are haunted objects. *Photo by Connie Hall-Scott.*

pivotal moment. Maybe it chose to go when staying would have been a better option or stayed when it should have gone, and the choice forever changed the course of its life. This spirit could be trying to rechoose through an act of repetition. The scenarios are endless, but the actual motivation will likely, as Rhonda Chastain said, remain a mystery to us.

In 2004, a group of paranormal researchers out of Atlanta known as the Foundation for Paranormal Research, or FPR, visited the Wink on two separate occasions through my invitation. They are a nonprofit, nonreligious, scientifically oriented investigative group specializing in ghosts and other phenomena that can be associated with the paranormal.

During their investigations, both small and large orbs were captured by digital cameras on stage, outside the projection room and in the Wink's basement. Orbs are defined as transparent or colored balls of lights that many believe to be a form of spirit energy. FPR captured a Class-A EVP, or electronic voice phenomenon, of a female in the balcony area just in front of the projection booth. The voice clearly said, "I see people."

The humor is not lost on me. Most of us who watched Bruce Willis in the 1999 movie *Sixth Sense* recall the kid, played by Haley Joel Osment, confessing, "I see dead people." It's a pretty popular quote with movie buffs. It could be that FPR captured the wit of a ghost through the medium of recording.

On the second of the two investigations, FPR used dowsing, or divining, rods. The copper rods, generally used to find underground water or unmarked graves, are a popular ghost-hunting tool. In theory, the two rods, when held in the still hands of an individual, will cross once contact with the other side has been made. At that point yes and no questions can be asked using a single rod. If the rod moves up and down, the spirit using the rod to communicate is believed to be saying yes. Likewise, if the rod moves from side to side, the spirit's answer is believed to be no. FPR is confident they made contact with a female spirit in the ladies' upstairs restroom using both the dowsing rods and a psychic. According to the psychic, there were eight spirits inside the theater on the night of the second investigation.

Mysterious hammerings, cold spots, orbs and EVPs, the lady in the bathroom, film randomly flying from reels, doorknobs turning by themselves, invisible playing children and unexplained noises all lend credit

The Wink is now owned by Rock Bridge Community Church. *Photo by Robert Hartline.*

to the probability that not all the persons patronizing the elegant three-story theater are of this world.

My father sold the Wink Theatre to Rock Bridge Community Church in 2005. Whether or not strange goings-on continue, I cannot say. My parents and other family members attend Sunday morning services there on a regular basis. I have myself attended a few and left feeling blessed. I encourage you to check it out for yourself if you haven't already. The Wink Theatre looms large at the center of West Crawford Street in historic downtown Dalton, a hop, skip and jump down from the bronze statue of Civil War hero general Joseph Johnston. Just look for the flashing marquee on Sunday mornings.

A Coffee Shop That Was Affected by the Wink's Renovation

Sometimes when a historic home or building undergoes restoration, paranormal activity reaches out into adjoining locations. Such is the case with the Wink Theatre and the coffee shop across the street. While there is currently such a coffee shop across from the Wink, it has a different name and is operated by different owners than when renovation of the theater was underway. In 2002, the building was owned by a local woman named Priscilla Mowles. She believed that ghosts from our theater visited her coffee shop.

Priscilla told me the original building on site was built in 1897 and used to house General Telephone. That building burned and was replaced by the one currently standing. She shared several events that took place in the Coffee Shop that left her and others more than a little baffled.

One of the stories she told me involves a cat she kept above the Coffee Shop in her private office. After renovation began at the Wink, her cat started to act "funny." The normally docile animal began to behave as if it were watching an invisible entity. The cat would hiss, run and hide for no discernible reason. On one of these occasions when her cat was unexplainably upset, Priscilla saw a white light flash by, and then the office door closed. This occurred around 9:00 p.m. The experience left her uneasy. It would happen again. Many times, Priscilla said, she felt as if someone was watching her while she worked in her office or downstairs in the shop.

Priscilla also told me about how an employee who worked in the Coffee Shop was troubled by something invisible pulling his shirt collar up on

The Coffee Shop as it is today, though it is now called the Perfect Cup. The owner of the building and employees who worked there when the Wink renovation began reported paranormal activity, which was believed to be linked to the theater. An interesting feature is the rooftop owl. *Photo by Connie Hall-Scott.*

more than one occasion. Similarly, a female employee was spooked by a mysterious pull on her apron. One time, a customer became agitated and demanded to know who had shoved him. Not only had no one in the room shoved him, but also no one in the room was even near him—no one still breathing anyway.

Priscilla talked about how the employees began getting stuck in the bathroom. Only when the stuck employee became upset, yelling and beating on the door, would the door open. She talked about how door chimes inside the window would swing from side to side when no one was close to them. The chimes were not near air-conditioning vents. There was no logical explanation, she said.

Priscilla's grandson Dallas Carter worked in the shop during the time of the disturbances. He shared, "You would feel a distinct tapping on your shoulder while knowing you were the only person in the shop. It also seemed to happen that every time you would walk to the kitchen, the front door chimes would jingle, and looking back out of the kitchen, you wouldn't see a single person in the dining area."

The business operating from the building now is the Perfect Cup.

In the spring of 2013, I began talking about the Wink Theatre to a group of ghost tour guests. As soon as I mentioned that the owner and employees of the Coffee Shop claimed they were affected by Wink renovation efforts, Lorrie Beth Martin spoke up.

"I used to work in downtown Dalton," Lorrie Beth shared. "I went to the Perfect Cup, across the street from the Wink Theatre, at least once a week for lunch. On one occasion, my friend and I were having lunch there when I needed to use the bathroom. When I tried to turn the handle to leave, the door would not open. It was almost as if someone was holding the knob on the other side, and the door was not locked. I pushed, pulled and shook but the door wouldn't open. At this point I started to get very agitated and a little nervous because I couldn't get out and I needed to get back to work. I finally pulled my phone out, and I was about to call my friend and ask her to come help me when I tried the door again and it opened right up. This happened in the fall of 2009."

CHAPTER TWO

THE WEEPING GIRL OF THE LANDMARK BUILDING

A couple years after I started Dalton Ghost Tours, I was leading a group along Hamilton Street when a lady spoke up.

"What do you know about the Landmark Building?" she inquired.

I began speaking of the great fire of 1911, of how the original Hotel Dalton had burned and about how a second hotel was built in its place and is now the Landmark Building. She stopped me.

"No, I mean, I think it's haunted," she alleged, going on to inform me that she and the person walking beside her worked on one of the middle floors and regularly experienced feelings of overwhelming sorrow and sadness and had even heard the faint weeping of an unseen female.

"We want to know who she is," her friend said. "No one likes to work late or be in the office alone."

That was the first I had heard of the weeping ghost of the Landmark Building. The year before, I had asked Randy Bates, local attorney and owner of the building, if he knew of any ghost stories or legends associated with the Landmark Building. He hadn't the first paranormal thing to share, at least at that time.

I was intrigued by what my two tour guests had to say about a possible weeping spirit. Not because they were the first to cry ghost but because it was evident the two of them were sincere and eager to learn more. I believed that they believed a spirit lingered inside their workplace. However, armed with no more information, I eventually forgot about the encounter—that is, until my dad and mom, Troy and Juanita Hall, embarked on one of my tours several years down the line. Neither of my parents—especially my dad—believes in earthbound spirits, but after the tour was over and my guests began to trickle away, my dad asked me a question.

"Did I ever tell you about the suicide I worked at the old hotel when I was a policeman?"

He had not. I was all ears.

In the late '60s and early '70s before he established Hall's Insurance Agency and Silver Leaf Tufters, Inc., my daddy served as a Dalton police officer. Turns out, he was one of the officers who responded to a call that went out from Hotel Dalton around 1968 or 1969. Unfortunately, I have been unable to pinpoint the exact date. Several people I have spoken with remember that it happened, just not exactly when it happened.

A young woman who worked as a carhop at the Cherokee Drive-in, formerly located on Cleveland Highway, checked in to Hotel Dalton one evening and shot herself. She was in the neighborhood of seventeen or eighteen years old and was distraught over a failed romance. My father's accounting of the incident painted a sad picture in my mind. What a waste of young life and potential. The story of the weeping presence described by those two ghost tour guests floated to the surface of my memory for the first time in a long time.

1970s promotional shot for WTTI radio at the Cherokee Drive-In. The young lady who took her life inside the Landmark Building worked at the Cherokee as a carhop. The three ladies shown are not connected to the suicide. *Photo by Steve Hill.*

In 2011, Atlanta psychic Victoria Bragg made a profound impression on me. It was her first visit to Dalton, though what she found here would bring her back a couple more times. As she and I walked across West Crawford Street, from the direction of the Wink Theatre toward the wooden deck that adjoins the Perfect Cup, she stopped dead in her tracks.

"What's that?" Victoria asked, pointing in the direction of the Landmark Building. "No wait, don't tell me. Let me tell you. Is it apartments? No, it's, it was, a hotel."

"That's right," I said. "How did you know?"

She gave me a look as if to remind me that she's psychic. I had just met her, though we'd talked over the phone a couple of times, and I maintained a healthy degree of skepticism. Maybe she had meandered over and read the little plaque on the front of the Landmark Building earlier, I briefly entertained. But she hadn't. I had arrived downtown while Victoria was still on the interstate traveling north toward Dalton, I reminded myself. I know this because we had been in communication by cellphone and my directions led her downtown.

Victoria was hyper focused on the Landmark Building.

"There's a young woman there right now," Victoria told me, a profound look of concern etched on her face. "She took her life there…she shot herself…she's very, very sad…a man was involved…he broke her heart and she felt like she couldn't go on without him…in the time-suspended split-second her finger applied pressure to the trigger, the full realization of what she was about to do hit her, and she didn't want to go through with the deed but it was already too late…"

I stared at Victoria with my mouth open. There's no way she could have had prior knowledge of what she was sharing because I had not disclosed what little information I possessed on the "weeping woman" with Victoria. No one has published anything about the suicide—until now—and Victoria had never so much as made a pit stop off Exit 333 to buy a Coke in Dalton, Georgia. In fact, she didn't know anyone in Dalton at that time, outside myself.

"The act occurred on either the second or third floor," Victoria continued. "Oh, my goodness!" For a moment, Victoria stood still, visibly distraught. "The poor girl was pregnant when she killed herself…she didn't know she was expecting, but she was…She likes to hang around the top portion of the building because she feels closer to God there. She's afraid to move on because of what she did, and she isn't sure if she'll receive forgiveness…She was generally a good girl and has communicated to me that she doesn't want

The Landmark Building today. *Photo by Angela Moss.*

to go to 'the bad place'…She's very lonely and eager to reach out to anyone who acknowledges her."

Since Victoria's revelation, I always talk about the weeping girl and what Victoria told me about her when leading paranormal seekers through the streets of historic downtown Dalton. More and more often, our ghost makes herself known, especially when there's a teenage girl or a young woman in her early twenties present who she seems to want to connect with. I think she's looking for a friend, a human connection.

One of the routes the ghost tour follows allows for a stop in front of the Landmark Building. While visitors look at Randy Bates's building, I share the tale of the weeping girl's tragedy. Public tours take place in the evening, normally when it's dark outside, and the Landmark Building is already closed for the day. All the lights are off inside. After a few minutes outside the Landmark Building, I proceed to lead the evening's group down to the Gordon Street Bridge for a visit with another of Dalton's lingering spirits. On our way back through, we again pass the Landmark Building. Sometimes the weeping girl has turned on a light or two for us.

Because this occurrence of the lights spontaneously coming on happens with more and more regularity, I asked Randy Bates if any of the building's lights are connected to timers and if anyone works at night. He answered no on both counts.

In early 2013, a group of six individuals booked a private ghost tour. Not one of my guests believed in ghosts. They were taking the tour solely to be entertained and to learn more about the history of Dalton. As I stood with my back to the Landmark Building, talking about the weeping girl, six sets of eyes looked at the building. I watched as a young lady in her late teens dropped her mouth as I had done when Victoria first channeled the weeping girl. This guest's eyes grew wide, and her face registered a combination of fascination and horror.

I turned to see what she was looking at, already knowing. A light on a middle floor illuminated a room.

"Did the light just…?"

"About two seconds ago," she answered as, at that very moment, a second light came on in a room down from the first.

There was a collective gasp, followed by doubting questions.

"How did you do that?" someone asked me.

"I didn't," I answered.

"Then who did?" someone else asked.

"I think you know the answer to that," I replied, though in truth I was already scanning the back of the building for cars of possible suspects. None was present. No other lights were on in the Landmark Building. No one was inside, unless you count the weeping girl.

"I think she did that for you," I told the young woman who first saw the light.

I can't say whether or not any of my previously nonbelieving guests left with changed beliefs concerning earthbound spirits that night, but I do believe they at least walked away with more open minds and questioning the possibility.

I have a friend who not long ago moved his office into a space in the Landmark Building. His wife soon contacted me to say they had experienced "something." Turns out while they were moving boxes and files into the office, someone unseen opened and shut doors around them. Maybe our weeping girl is simply, like Victoria Bragg said, eager to make her presence known.

Located at 101 East Crawford Street, the Landmark Building is a five-floor low-rise. Finished in 1923, it has been on the National Register of Historic Places since 1988.

CHAPTER THREE

CHEROKEE INDIANS

HERE FIRST, HERE STILL?

Until the mid-1700s, the area of present-day Dalton was inhabited by Woodland and Creek Indians. Cherokee Indians soon pushed those peoples to the west and south and took root. The Cherokees referred to the mountains of North Georgia as their "Enchanted Land." For many years, they thrived and were a happy people. Their fortune would turn, however, delivering to them unspeakable violence, pain and suffering. Acts such as those committed on the soils where the proud Cherokees dwelled left a gaping wound in history and, some believe, the occasional disgruntled spirit.

I have been told by local historians that the area on which the Whitfield County Courthouse sits, at 300 West Crawford Street, was used by the Cherokee as a playing field and for ceremonies.

The Cherokees played ball to determine which village reigned supreme in the art of mayhem on the field. Two teams, representing their respective villages, would gather on the field and set up goal posts at each end. The midpoint between each goal post was marked. The teams would then pair off into opponents, and the referee would throw the ball up between the two captains.

Anything went—biting, choking, gouging, scratching, twisting of arms and legs and even hitting each other over the head with wooden rackets. The idea of the game was to carry the ball between the goal posts twelve times. The first team to have twelve pegs stuck in the ground by the medicine man would win. Timeouts and substitutions were not allowed. The game went on until twelve pegs were in the ground. Twenty men might start the game and

Whitfield County Courthouse today. *Photo by Angela Moss.*

only a few finish it. Indians from miles away would gather to watch a game, betting personal possessions on their athletes of choice.

The Cherokee worked hard, and they played hard, sometimes to the death.

On psychic Victoria Bragg's first visit to Dalton, she accompanied me to the Wink Theatre. Standing in front of the building she said, "The story you told me about Leon Hurst hearing children with bells on their feet outside his office in this theater is half correct—he did hear bells, and others have heard the bells; but those bells weren't attached to the shoes of young children. They were affixed to the ankles of Indians who danced in ceremonies held very near here."

I had not mentioned Indians to Victoria before she shared that piece of information with me, and she was unversed in the history of Whitfield County.

"There are native spirits who visit from time to time," she said. "A lot of energy was released on this land. A lot of things happened here both good and bad."

The Cherokees who lived in Whitfield County were members of the Chelsea Cherokee Nation. By 1800, the Cherokees had begun assimilating with implanted white settlers. The Cherokees farmed, raised animals and established blacksmith services, stores and mills. Many of them had even adopted the white man's religious beliefs and were educated through Moravian mission schools.

A prosperous Cherokee called Youngbird (1817–1837) lived at Hamilton Spring, northwest of the spring. His house was a double log cabin with stone chimneys. He raised horses coveted by Indians and white men alike. Youngbird spent a lot of his time racing. One of his favorite places to run his horses was the length of what is now Thornton Avenue. On one of his wild rides, Youngbird was thrown from his most cherished horse. He died from the injuries and was buried, along with his horse, in the downtown Dalton area.

That might have been the end of Youngbird's story, but it wasn't. Legend has it that Youngbird's spirit is upset by what happened to his people and by what happened to his own remains.

We'll start with what happened to his people.

One year after Youngbird's death ride, in 1838, the United States government forced the removal of the Cherokee from their Enchanted Land through a holocaust that would become known as the Trail of Tears. Indians were removed not only from Whitfield County and other parts of Georgia but also from South Carolina, North Carolina, Tennessee, Texas and Alabama. It seems settlers wanted not only the Cherokees' land but also the gold that was believed to come with their land. Still

Modern-day Cherokees playing ball, as they did in the area of today's Whitfield County Courthouse before their removal. In actuality, the game was brutal. *Photo courtesy of Cherokee Heritage Center.*

This monument is dedicated to the memory of Youngbird, who once owned the land on which it sits, behind Crown Gardens & Archives. It is not a grave marker. *Photo by Connie Hall-Scott.*

today, people talk about and hunt for the "lost Cherokee gold" in and around North Georgia.

Private John G. Burnett of Captain Abraham McClellan's Company, Second Regiment, Second Brigade, was a firsthand witness to the horrors of the Trail of Tears. Able to speak the Cherokee language fluently, Private Burnett was utilized as an interpreter. He wrote about those horrific days on his eightieth birthday, and his account has been retold in numerous publications since.

"I saw the helpless Cherokees arrested and dragged from their homes, and driven at bayonet point into the stockades. And in the chill of a drizzling rain on an October morning I saw them loaded like cattle and sheep into 645 wagons and started toward the west," he recorded.

Not all the Cherokees had blankets, and many were driven from home without shoes on their feet. In fact, not all of them were "lucky" enough to have been loaded into wagons; some were forced to walk through sleet and snow and freezing temperatures.

"The suffering of the Cherokee was awful," Private Burnett wrote. "The trail of the exiles was a trail of death. They had to sleep in the wagons and on the ground without fire. I have known as many as 22 of them to die in one night of pneumonia due to ill treatment, cold and exposure."

Bodies were buried in shallow graves along the way. Sometimes the dead weren't buried at all. The long journey to the West ended in March 1839 with four thousand dead reaching from the foothills of the Smoky Mountains to what is now Oklahoma.

"Crimes were committed that were a disgrace to civilization," Private Burnett surmised.

He wrote of men who were shot in cold blood, homes that were burned, men working in fields who were arrested and women who were dragged from their homes by soldiers whose language they could not understand. He told of children who were separated from their parents and driven into the stockades with but the sky for a blanket and the earth for a pillow and of how the old and infirm were prodded with bayonets.

"Is there any wonder spirits were left behind?" commented former Daltonian Samantha Turner, whose great-great-grandmother was full Cherokee. "The stockades were concentration camps. There was much prejudice against the Indians and they were rarely treated with kindness or with respect as they were herded along. It's too sad for me to think about."

Once the Cherokees were removed from what would become Dalton, work began on an important new frontier: the American railroad. The Western & Atlantic (W&A) rail linked the Tennessee River with cities near the Chattahoochee. Once completed in 1850, a second rail to connect East Tennessee to Georgia was created. More people came and settled.

Those tracks were laid over the resting place of Youngbird and his horse. There are some who say his spirit is none too happy about it.

"There have been wrecks where he's buried," an elderly resident of Whitfield County proclaimed in the spring of 2013, "car wrecks and train wrecks. Train conductors have seen mystery lights when passing over his body, and those red and white lights follow them a ways down the track. People used to talk about all that. I guess Youngbird didn't like having his grave site desecrated. I can't say I'd like it either."

"My granddaddy used to tell of how people have seen the ghost of Youngbird riding atop his horse whipping to and fro in the place where his body is buried," he went on to say. "Granddaddy claimed a fella he knew swore up and down he saw the ghost of Youngbird's horse stand up on its hind legs, the Indian on top of it, right there at the tracks late one night."

Local historian Marcelle White once told me she heard that a train derailed near Youngbird's grave, but she isn't sure how accurate the claim is. In fact, according to railroad accident reports, a derailment did occur in Dalton on June 12, 1912. The result was four fatalities and sixty-four

Georgia's state flower, the Cherokee rose, has symbolism and lore tied to the Trail of Tears. *Photo by Connie Hall-Scott.*

injuries. A memorandum from the chief inspector states the cause as "excessive speed over a bad section of track." Yet later in the report, he contradicts himself by describing the track section as "well-maintained."

"I've heard of Youngbird's ghost," Tara Smith-Linville of Tunnel Hill said. "He's buried under the railroad tracks downtown, right?"

That does seem to be the case if local legend is to be believed, though the exact location of his body is hard to pinpoint. A monument has been placed behind Crown Gardens & Archives, located at 715 Chattanooga Avenue in Dalton, near where he lived.

As every good Georgian knows, the Cherokee rose is our official state flower. It is a perfect symbol of the pain and suffering brought about by the Trail of Tears. There's a legend associated with this lovely flower. It's said that the mothers of the Cherokee grieved so much that the chiefs prayed for a sign to lift their spirits and give them strength to care for their little ones. From the time of the prayer, a beautiful new flower—the Cherokee rose—grew wherever a mother's tear fell to the ground. The rose is white for the women's tears. It has a gold center for the gold taken from the Cherokee lands. It has seven leaves on each stem to represent the seven Cherokee clans that made the journey. The Cherokee rose still thrives along the route of the Trail of Tears. Whenever I see a Cherokee rose, I am always reminded of the heart-wrenching plight of the Cherokee.

Nearby Dalton, Red Clay State Park, New Echota and the Chief Vann House stand as additional reminders of the Cherokee people who once loved the land of North Georgia.

CHAPTER FOUR

HOLLY TREE HOUSE HAUNTING

Placing gargoyles atop buildings and outside dwellings to ward off evil spirits and provide protection is a tradition that began in France centuries ago. Such carvings guard the entrance of the Holly Tree House, located at 217 West Cuyler Street, though they haven't exactly kept the spirits out according to some of the folks who've spent time there.

The two-story white home with black shutter–adorned windows was built in 1924 for the Gravitt family. Mr. Gravitt was the first general manager of the American Thread Company of New England. Julian and Mary B. Longley purchased the home in 1938 and resided there for five decades. In 1993, it was purchased by Doris Fiorito of California and her daughter Katie Soesbee, whom locals know as a proprietor of popular restaurant the Spiced Apple.

Once upon a time, Doris told me that she and Katie consulted with people who had visited the Holly Tree House "in the day" before restoring the dwelling as closely as possible to what it used to be. Together, they created an impressive atmosphere by accentuating the historic craftsmanship, such as the inlaid wood floors and original architecture, and incorporating modern conveniences.

For years, the home served as a bed-and-breakfast and welcomed guests like the late actor and National Rifle Association activist Charlton Heston.

"It was so odd to find yourself sitting across from Moses at the breakfast table," Doris told me. "He liked bagels and peanut butter. He was raising money for the Republican Party at the time."

This gargoyle guards the entrance of historic Holly Tree House. *Photo by Angela Moss.*

The Holly Tree House is one of the oldest residential homes in downtown Dalton. *Photo by Angela Moss.*

Senator Phil Graham from Texas, who once ran for president, stayed up eating pie 'til midnight at the Holly Tree House. Representative Bob Barr slept there, and so did a team representing Italy for the Tour de France bike race that used to run through Dalton.

"The girl who skied the Olympics with the artificial leg [Bonnie St. John] stayed with us," Doris said. "She ran up and down the stairs. Such an impressive young lady!"

Guests have been known to ask if the house is haunted after a night's stay.

One of Doris's daughters told her she believes there's an otherworldly presence in the house.

"When she visited from California, she told me she ran from the landing to her room upstairs," Doris shared. "I asked her if she was frightened, and she told me she wasn't but that she still didn't like to be around whatever is there. She said that once she got inside her room she felt fine."

Doris believes her ghost might be that of the gentleman who originally lived there.

Left: The closed door leads to the basement of the Holly Tree House. It is in front of this door that phantom cigar smoke has been smelled. The curio in front of the door holds part of a doll collection started by Doris Fiorito. *Photo by Connie Hall-Scott.*

Below: The open doorway leads to the bedroom that offers haven from Holly Tree House ghosts, according to a former owner's daughter. *Photo by Connie Hall-Scott.*

"When I walk from the kitchen to the bedroom I can sometimes smell cigar smoke even though no one smokes here," she said. "I smell it outside the door to the basement that I believe was his workshop. I've smelled it around twelve times."

"I have spoken with some elderly ladies who knew the family who lived here, and they liked them very much," she went on to say. "Evidence points to this having been a very happy home."

Visitors from as far away as England and New Zealand have booked stays and return stays at the Holly Tree Inn, where they enjoyed gourmet breakfasts and beautiful surroundings.

Those beautiful surroundings could provide answers to why some believe the Holly Tree Inn offers lodging not only to the living but also to the once living. Just as Rhonda Chastain believes the original Wink Theatre doors came with ghostly strings, it could be that the oodles and oodles of interesting objects from around the world and collections from family heirlooms housed within the Holly Tree House have some spectral hangers-on.

This opulent house was designed and decorated to spark guests' imaginations as much as to provide comfort and relaxation. Each room was put together with a specific motif in mind and arouses one's curiosity just by their names. There's the Normandy Room, the Savannah Room, the Hampton Room, the St. Ives Room and the Seville Room.

Many of the collections began long ago, such as the dolls Doris started acquiring when she was four years old. The first was a Shirley Temple doll that remains in good shape. Incidentally, Doris accompanied her family on a cruise during the Depression years and spent time playing with the little movie star.

Doris kept dolls from her trip to Hawaii when she was five years old and began a full-on foreign collection in her twenties. The collection swelled to include little darlings from Morocco, England, Scotland, Wales, Ireland, France, Italy, Spain, Portugal, the Netherlands, Belgium, Switzerland, Mexico and other faraway places. Doris didn't stop acquiring until her curio was full. Some of the dolls are over one hundred years old. There's a set of hand-carved monks picked up in Turkey. There are twenty "Famous American Women" dolls, including caricatures of Eleanor Roosevelt, Betsy Ross, Pocahontas, Abigail Adams and Dolley Madison. Handmade marionettes were picked up in Paris, portraying the phantom from the *Phantom of the Opera* and a female who Doris said "looks like she would be tending bar in the lower part of Paris."

There are hundreds of stories about haunted dolls out there. Forget about Chucky from the horror classic *Child's Play*. The real terror comes in learning about alleged real-life spirit-to-doll attachments.

Robert the Doll, an infamous resident of the Fort East Martello Museum in Key West, Florida, is a prime example. Given to Robert Eugene Otto in 1906 by a vengeful Bahamian servant who practiced black magic, the doll was actually heard talking by young Robert's parents. Neighbors claimed to have seen the doll moving from window to window. Friends heard it omit a terrifying giggle, and handfuls of people claim to have witnessed it run from room to room. The story of Robert the Doll escalates and grows darker, but that's a tale for other books. I mention it merely to provide one of countless examples of haunted doll accounts. If one or more of Doris's dolls has paranormal presence, it or they don't seem to be anything like Robert or Chucky.

Other collections of the Holly Tree Inn include lovely glass dishes, produced in the 1920s and 1930s, originally owned by Doris's mother. And there are the Lilliput Lane houses, exact replicas of houses in England that were picked up in the motherland, as well as lots of other fascinating items placed about in different rooms.

So far as we know, the ghost or ghosts at the Holly Tree House fall under the category of friendly. No harm has been done outside frightening a person here and a person there. Whether former occupants or object-attached spirits, these specters certainly add flavor to one of Dalton's oldest residential homes.

CHAPTER FIVE

THE HANGED AND THE LYNCHED

A MURDERER, HIS CAT AND A CURSE

The difference between a hanging and a lynching is simply that one is legal and the other isn't. Dalton has hosted but one legalized hanging. It occurred on September 11, 1914, at 11:00 a.m., in unison with the courthouse bell. According to some superstitious citizens, the killer who was hanged left behind a grieving friend and a curse.

W.I. Umphrey was hanged for the murder of sixty-year-old Joseph Pritchett. A veteran of the Civil War, Umphrey eventually made his way down south in search of work. He settled in Dalton where he became a tenant of Joseph Pritchett's farm in Varnell.

The *North Georgia Citizen* described Joseph Pritchett as one of Whitfield County's "good, substantial farmers" who was "held in high esteem of his neighbors." Although not a rich man, Pritchett owned considerable property and lived comfortably.

As bad luck would have it, a dispute arose between Umphrey and Pritchett over the division of a bale of cotton, resulting in Umphrey uttering threats against Pritchett. Pritchett took the threats seriously enough to procure a peace warrant. In an attempt to end the heated quarrel, friends of both men stepped in and held mediation. The cotton was divided, and Pritchett withdrew his warrant.

But Umphrey was not satisfied. Henry Brooker, J.B. Walker, Ed Caylor and other witnesses swore that Umphrey claimed he intended to have the eighteen dollars he felt he'd been cheated of, one way or another. "Dead men tell no tales," Umphrey is said to have threatened. Additionally, Umphrey approached Constable Tom Gilbert three days before Pritchett was killed, saying he was going to South Georgia and "if anything happens to Pritchett, don't try to pack it off on me."

Shortly after 1:00 p.m. on a Monday, Joseph Pritchett went to the woodpile near his house. His intent was to haul wood into town to sell. Pritchett's prolonged absence caused the family concern, and his eleven-year-old granddaughter, Zella Witherspoon, was sent out to look for him. The child found her grandfather's lifeless body near his wagon; he'd never made it to Dalton.

Local officers with bloodhounds hurried to the scene. The town was shocked by the atrociousness of the crime, for the murderer, not satisfied with ambushing his victim, waited until Pritchett's back was turned before firing on him with a shotgun. Bullets entered the victim's head and neck. Pritchett never saw it coming.

The bloodhounds quickly picked up a scent and held it until they reached a private road leading to the home of John Underwood, where Umphrey boarded. Officers found their suspect at the Butler family's store in north Dalton. Instead of denying his guilt, Umphrey said, "They'll have to prove it."

A mountain of circumstantial evidence was presented at Umphrey's jury trial. He was found guilty, and Judge Fite sentenced him to be "hanged by the neck until he is dead, dead, dead."

It rained on the day of Umphrey's execution. Dark clouds hung over Dalton as several hundred people gathered on the lawns outside the Whitfield County Courthouse and jail. Attracted by morbid curiosity, the crowd was eager to catch even a fleeting glimpse of some minor detail of the execution as they watched the large minute hand on the clock in the tower of the courthouse.

As the clock ticked off minutes, the Reverend O.D. Flaming, pastor of the First Baptist Church, prayed with the prisoner. Dressed in an inexpensive suit bought for him by the town, Umphrey was given his last shave before county deputies entered his cell.

It is said that W.I. Umphrey walked to the gallows unshaken and without tremor. The event of his death was to take place within the walls of the county jail with a handful of officers, the undertaker, three doctors and Reverend Flaming in attendance. At the request of Umphrey, a young boy by the name of Bill Birch was permitted to witness the execution. Birch had been kind to Umphrey during his stay in jail, and Umphrey wanted his hanging to "prove a lasting lesson" for the boy.

Since the beginning of his incarceration, Umphrey had shared his cell with a cat. On the day of the execution, while officers tied Umphrey's feet together, they repeatedly had to brush the cat aside.

Strangely enough, sometimes when a ghost tour group embarks on a walk through historic downtown, we see a cat cross King Street in the vicinity of the courthouse.

"I've taken the tour several times, and I think that cat has been there every time," remarked Nick Michael of Rocky Face. "It's a little creepy because it always makes an appearance as the guide is speaking of that hanging and then it's gone. It's never close enough to see exactly what it looks like, and it's never there for long."

On a couple of occasions, I've had tour guests ask where "the cat" went.

"What cat?" I ask, only to be told a cat had been rubbing up against some guest's ankles. Downtown Dalton isn't exactly overrun by wild or domesticated cats. It's not often you'll see a cat downtown, except maybe when talking about W.I. Umphrey.

"I think it's the spirit of the hanged man's cat friend," Nick Michael opined. "If people can be ghosts, why can't animals be ghosts?"

According to Mary Ann Winkowski, author of *When Ghosts Speak: Understanding the World of Earthbound Spirits*, animals indeed can and sometimes do remain earthbound for a while. Mary Ann is an acclaimed paranormal investigator. The Melinda Ellis character from the series *Ghost Whisperer* was based on Mary Ann's real life.

"When they die, most animals will instinctively go into the white light, knowing they have fulfilled their purpose on earth," Mary Ann claims. "But for some animals, loyalties may override their instincts, causing them to choose to remain earthbound."

"Tell the world they are killing an innocent man," Umphrey told his death entourage.

The convicted murderer was allowed one final glimpse of the dismal Georgia day before a black hood was placed over his head. "God, receive me," were his final words before the clock tolled off the hour.

Eleven full strokes of the bell sounded before the harsh clang of the iron doors fell apart to make the opening through which the victim dropped. Umphrey's faithful cat friend had joined in his death march and took its place on the scaffold with the prisoner. When the trapdoor opened, the cat took the death plunge along with its master.

The crowd pushed toward the jail, many scrambling for a place at the window through which they could view the swaying body of W.I. Umphrey. Aside from one slight convulsive heave of the shoulders, Umphrey's body remained stationary. When his body was cut down and placed in the coffin, the cat followed it to the undertaker's wagon, after which it returned to the jail and began searching for Umphrey.

It could be that the feline is still searching, even now, one hundred years after Umphrey's demise. If so, that's serious loyalty.

Once, I noticed another distracted tour guest looking around the ground, as if she, too, were searching for something. Not only was she distracted, but she was also distracting those around her with her fidgety glances and a series of loud sneezes. I suspected she'd dropped something and continued my spiel. When I came to the part about W.I. Umphrey's cat, she spoke up.

"You've got to be kidding me," she said, grabbing hold of the arm of her companion. "There could be a spirit cat here?"

Turned out, my guest was allergic to cats and was experiencing symptoms of her allergy. She hadn't been looking for an earring or a bracelet but for a cat.

In 2004, I spoke with Helen Meers, a descendant of Umphrey's victim Joseph Pritchett. Helen told me about another tragedy that struck the farm where Joseph met his end. It seems a body was found in an old well on the farm in the 1980s. She learned of the incident by reading an article submitted by Harold Cardwell Sr. in the *Official History of Whitfield County*.

"When I was in high school I used to ride out to where the farm was, way down Broadacre Road, for cheap thrills," Ron Chastain of Tunnel Hill recalled with a chuckle. "I had heard it was cursed land and that someone had been killed there a long time ago. I didn't know if it was true or not at the time—still don't—but I can tell you it gave me the willies. It could be that bad mojo was left behind. That's what they say anyway."

W.I. Umphrey lies in an unmarked grave at West Hill Cemetery. Joseph Pritchett's body rests at Grove Level Baptist Church on Cleveland Highway, near his old farm. As for the cat, maybe you'll be one of the chosen ones to feel it sweeping up against your ankles if you find yourself in the historic district some night.

THE DESPERATE SPIRIT OF A LYNCHED MAN

Like most old American towns, Dalton has experienced its share of mob justice resulting in the accused dangling at the end of a rope. Some older area citizens still remember seeing a poor soul hanging from a tree, a rooftop or a bridge.

To this day, a framed photograph of a man hanging from the Gordon Street Bridge dots a wall in a downtown barbershop, a solemn reminder of a violent ending. The shot was taken in July 1907, and it ran in the *Dalton Argus* on the front page. Around the hanged man stand a crowd of onlookers, all male, ranging from childhood to the middle aged. It's hard to tell what they were thinking, though none of them looks upset about the dead man.

Doc Posey was hated, having committed a deed referred to in the newspaper as "the most horrible crime that ever occurred in this county."

In 2009, I instructed a follow-up course to a wildly popular continuing education class I had taught along with Drew Hester at Dalton State College called Ghostbusting 101. The new class, Ghostbusting 102, took participants deeper into the world of the paranormal and offered field experience. For our first outing, I took the class to historic downtown Dalton, where we broke off into groups and explored many of the sites mentioned in this book, as well as a few private locations. Some of the most interesting activity occurred in the area of the Gordon Street Bridge.

My students already knew the story of Doc Posey and were armed with various instruments including digital cameras and recorders, EMF readers, spirit rods and open minds. I had also invited along with us psychic Victoria Bragg. As a group walked toward the bridge, student Missy Nelson and I conversed with Victoria.

All at once, Victoria stopped walking and grabbed her stomach.

"Are you okay?" we asked.

"I don't feel good," she answered. "It's my stomach. I just need a minute."

As we stood there, Victoria began to tell us she was feeling the sorrow of a hanged man. He felt, she said, like he was wrongly hanged. But wait, that's not the extraordinary part. Most individuals facing the noose probably feel they should not be hanged, regardless of guilt or innocence. The extraordinary factor entered the evening when a husband and wife from the class ran up to us with their digital camera yelling, "Look at this!"

Within the frame of their camera, we saw Missy, myself and Victoria. Train tracks were to the side of us, and the Gordon Street Bridge provided backdrop. Missy wore a look of concern for Victoria on her face, and I was caught midsentence. Victoria stood with one hand on her stomach and the other gesturing in conjunction with her speech. Above Victoria's head loomed a very clear, perfect ectoplasm of a large hand reaching down.

An ectoplasm is the ghostly substance that issues from a medium who is communicating with spirits. The hand above Victoria's head was formed of white mist. Five fingers were splayed out, reaching downward from the palm in the direction of Victoria's head. Features of the hand were evident, from the bones and joints of the fingers to the proportions. Above the hand, the wrist could be seen along with about four inches of arm. From the fingers escaped light dewy bolts as if feeding into Victoria's consciousness.

The captured image alone would be profound. The timing made it even more so, as the image was captured at the same time Victoria channeled the hanged man.

"I've never seen anything like that before," Victoria said of the image, clearly fascinated. "I've seen a lot of things, but this is right up there."

Victoria didn't tell us much about the hanged man outside his feeling cheated, stuck, sad and terrified. She said he had been a horse thief, which is interesting because I had not included that information when speaking to the class. I didn't feel it especially relevant since that was not the crime Doc Posey was hanged for. Yet Marcelle White, formerly of the Whitfield-Murray Historical Society, had told me Posey was a known horse thief.

Here's his story:

Thirty-five-year-old Doc Posey moved from Walker County to Rocky Face about two weeks before he was lynched. His fate was sealed once he coolly carried his nine-year-old, terribly battered stepdaughter into Dalton on a Saturday, claiming other parties had assaulted her. His actions were suspicious, so he was taken into custody by Officer Jackson and locked up.

His wife came into town, and the child, in critical condition, named Posey as the culprit. On Sunday, Posey made a complete confession in the presence of Deputy Sheriff Sam C. Britton and Reverend W.H. Bird.

B.L. Heartsill, editor and proprietor of the *Dalton Argus*, wrote of Posey's confession in the July 6, 1907 edition, saying, "He went into details and told them how he carried the little child into an old field and accomplished his purpose, and where they would find a part of his clothing which was used to conceal the crime. Later a search was made and the bloody clothing found and everything as he had described."

The field is about four miles north of Dalton, near Hassler's Mill.

The nature and ferocity of the crime struck the town with horror, and as news of the confession leaked out, a mob formed. Around 1:30 a.m., a group of between twenty-five and thirty men wearing long black robes with masks that came to a point on top barged into the jail housing Posey and demanded the prisoner at gun point. Deputy Britton, Reverend Bird, Officer Horton and Officer Moreland had no choice but to comply. Posey's hands were tied behind his back, and he was taken by a buggy in the direction of Hamilton Street to the Gordon Street Bridge.

Witnesses say the leader of the mob was the only one to speak but that all the men seemed to be "gentlemen" as not one curse word was uttered as a protesting Posey was strung up.

"He was terribly frightened and when commanded to walk his legs gave way and several were forced to carry him," one witness said. "He was asked if he committed the crime, the leader of the crowd stating that they did not want to hang an innocent man. Posey acknowledged that he was guilty but pitifully begged them to spare his life for a time, as he was not prepared to die. He was given 15 minutes to pray before the buggy pulled out from under him and he slowly strangled to death."

By the time Deputy Britton reached the home of Sheriff Johnson and the two of them made their way to the Gordon Street Bridge, it was too late to attempt any sort of intervention. Officers Horton and Moreland

The Gordon Street Bridge, from which Doc Posey was lynched, can be seen in the distance beyond the train tracks that run parallel to Hamilton Street in historic downtown Dalton. *Photo by Angela Moss.*

had been forced to accompany the mob but were peacefully released after the task was complete.

By 6:30 a.m. Monday morning, Posey's body was cut down in front of a gathered crowd.

Posey's wife wanted nothing to do with his body, so it was embalmed and put on a train to be delivered to the Anatomical Board of Health in Atlanta on that very night. It seems the townspeople couldn't get Posey out fast enough.

According to the *Dalton Argus*, Deputy Britton stated, "If it were possible to say, after knowing all the facts and hearing Posey's confession, and to publish it just as I heard him confess, it would shock the whole world to know that such a man lived as long as he did before meeting his fate."

A few other bizarre things happened at the Gordon Street Bridge on the night the Ghostbusting 102 class investigated. For one, when taking photos of a reportedly haunted site in hopes of getting evidence, it's important to take a series of photographs as opposed to just one. This allows you to see the movement and progression of an ectoplasm, orb or entity. One team was able to capture with its digital camera the formation of a red rope through a series of shots. The images showed the rope coming over the side of the bridge, going down and finishing with a noose. No image of a body within the rope was visible.

The current bridge replaced the wooden bridge that existed in 1907.

Additionally, one male Ghostbusting 102 student who had felt fine prior to the bridge investigation suddenly grew ill and nervous. He vomited on site and developed a pounding headache. After leaving the location, he once again was fine.

"I think Posey feels he should have been forgiven for what he did," Victoria surmised. "He still can't believe they did that to him. It seems he doesn't want to move on to what's next out of fear for what may await him."

The Gordon Street Bridge connects Hamilton Street and Glenwood Avenue. Train tracks run beneath it. I don't advise curiosity seekers to explore the area alone or at night.

CHAPTER SIX

DALTON LITTLE THEATRE'S HAUNTED HOST

The two-story brick building located at 210 North Pentz Street in historic downtown Dalton is home to Georgia's oldest performing community theater. And for over half a century, it has also lodged a mischievous ghost known as "Carl."

Dalton Little Theatre, or DLT, has entertained North Georgia with live performances since 1869, only breaking for World War I and World War II. But before the structure housed DLT, it served as a fire hall and is often still referred to as "the Old Firehouse." Two green awnings attach to the face of the building under which onlookers can make out the dual openings where fire wagons pulled by horses, and later more modern fire engines, were kept until called to duty.

It's not surprising that this place holds a great deal of residual energy. High emotions have played out inside the walls of the Old Firehouse for as long as it has existed. Imagine, if you will, the firefighters who spent time together there—joking and laughing, sharing meals, feeling the adrenaline rush that must have come when they were called out to tame raging fires, perhaps even with anxiety and a little fear. And let's not forget the sadness they must have felt for the occasional person they could not save.

These days it isn't firemen filling the building with emotion but artists and patrons. The actors who perform with Dalton Little Theatre reach deep inside themselves, often extracting expressions of extreme emotion—despair, hilarity, love, betrayal, malice, joy—eliciting strong

Dalton Little Theatre, a white building with green awnings, is home to a ghost called Carl. *Photo by Connie Hall-Scott.*

reactions from those who regularly come to see their shows. Many of the actors, directors, crew and even patrons know, as several of the firemen before them knew, Carl.

I first heard about Carl through mumblings of actors performing in theatrical productions at the Wink Theatre when I worked there. Naturally, some of those acting in plays at the Wink had acted in productions at Dalton Little Theatre. I learned from these thespians that Carl Johnson had been a fireman at the Old Firehouse back in the 1950s. It is said that he and his fellow firemen were called on to put out a fire. After the job was done, they returned to the firehouse. As was their routine, they all went upstairs to shower and change clothes. Everyone went upstairs except Carl. He is said to have told the others that he didn't feel well and was going to rest a bit. When the firemen came back downstairs, they found Carl in his favorite chair, asleep, or so they assumed. As time passed and Carl remained still and quiet, someone went to rouse him, only to discover he was dead. He had died from a heart attack.

According to the popular tale, Carl was laid to rest. Shortly thereafter, people in the firehouse began to report strange occurrences. Some firemen said they saw a man who looked like Carl out of the corners of their eyes, but upon turning to face him, he would be gone. Others claimed to see a fast-moving shadow figure. A few believe they came face to face with his apparition and witnessed it disappear before their eyes.

After putting out fires or going through drills, the firemen continued to come back to the firehouse and go immediately upstairs to shower and dress. The next step of their routine entailed returning downstairs to clean and put away equipment. After Carl's passing, a surprising ritual began to occur. It is said that once downstairs, the men would find that fire hoses had been wound and things put away. Yet no one was downstairs to wind the hoses or put away equipment. Nor would anyone have had time to do it all even if someone had been downstairs. They said Carl did it.

Later, after all the firemen moved on to a larger location and Dalton Little Theatre moved into the building on Pentz Street, Carl stayed. According to more than a few, he's pretty active.

A woman who was directing a production at DLT once told me a story about how she and a friend were creating a set. On a dining table, they placed plates, silverware, cloth napkins, a floral arrangement and glasses. Together, the two left the building late that evening. The next morning, the two met outside, bright and early, to resume set preparation. The director unlocked the door, and inside they went. What they found sent chills up their spines and raised a lot of questions.

The floral arrangement had been knocked over. The plates, silverware, glasses and cloth napkins were heaped atop the overturned arrangement,

Dalton Little Theatre, up close. Dalton Ghost Tour guests have taken a lot of photos showing orbs around the upstairs windows. *Photo by Angela Moss.*

and the four chairs that had been around the table were neatly pushed back about two feet from the table.

"No one had been to the theater within the time my companion and I left it and when we went back," she told me. "Believe me, I asked around. I often felt like I was being watched inside DLT, and it wasn't uncommon for the lights and sound system to do funky things during performances. I'll admit that sometimes I felt scared to be in areas of the building alone."

I have attended productions at DLT since the 1990s and always enjoyed my time there. I was pleasantly surprised when my daughter, Lexi, asked if she could audition for local teenager Amy Hartline's production of *A Christmas Story* in 2010. I took her, along with her brother Adam, to auditions held upstairs at DLT. Adam got bored right off the bat.

"When can we leave?" he mumbled to me over and over.

"Is this almost over?" he wanted to know.

Then, finally, he told me he needed to step outside to adjust his contact lens. When he came back in the room, he seemed thoughtful. Once we left the building, he told me why.

"Did an old man go into the room you were in?" he asked.

"No, why?" I asked.

"Something kind of freaked me out in there," Adam said.

Before I recount what my then twelve-year-old son shared with me, I remind my readers that I operate a ghost tour in Dalton. On the tour we talk about Dalton Little Theatre and Carl. However, neither Adam nor his twin brother, Aaron, is the least bit interested in Dalton Ghost Tours or the stories told. I can't recall a time the boys attended a tour with me that they actually listened to anything I had to say or even stuck close to the tour group. So what I'm trying to say here is that Adam didn't know or care who Carl was.

Adam said he stopped at the top of the staircase, took his contact lens out, wet it and began putting it back in his eye.

"I moved over to the side so the man walking up could pass me," he said. "When my contact was in I looked up and the guy was gone."

"I think you had a Carl experience," I said excitedly. I told him about Carl, and he was less enthused than I was. He wasn't scared, but he remained thoughtful.

Adam described the man he saw as "old," though to tweens and teens thirty looks old so my son's description is subjective. He also said Carl was "dressed weird," in shorts with suspenders and a white T-shirt with dark socks and dress shoes, a clothing choice appropriate for a '50s-era fireman on duty but at leisure, I submit.

I got to know Carl a little better when I signed on to direct the deliciously southern and decadent Tennessee Williams play *Cat on a Hot Tin Roof* in 2011. Once rehearsals began, the inevitable mention of Carl soon followed. Often, people associated with DLT will blame Carl when something goes missing—a prop, a paint brush, a costume. No one really believes Carl is responsible; the accusation is thrown out as a way of saying, "Who knows what happened."

Other times though, Carl does seem to make his presence known. One night Drew Hester stopped by DLT to take some publicity shots for *Cat on a Hot Tin Roof*. After the actors left, Drew, my stage director Missy Nelson, my son Aaron and I worked on the set a while. Approaching midnight, we were all tired and ready for bed. Instead of leaving immediately, we sat in the auditorium and talked. Drew and I have explored a number of reportedly haunted locations together, so naturally the conversation drifted to Carl.

As I recounted how our mutual friend Reese Christian, psychic medium and author of *Ghosts of Atlanta: Phantoms of the Phoenix City*, had

One of the dressing rooms behind the stage at Dalton Little Theatre. Sometimes when things go missing, as they often do, actors and volunteers like to blame DLT's ghost, Carl. *Photo by Robert Hartline.*

A promotional shot of the cast of Connie Hall-Scott's version of Tennessee Williams's sultry play *Cat on a Hot Tin Roof*, performed at DLT in 2011. Several cast members and volunteers experienced the antics of Carl during the putting together of this production. *Photo by Margaret Zeisig.*

told me the year before while a guest of Dalton Ghost Tours that Carl was "the equivalent of a ghost gone mad," the four of us heard the distinct sound of walking on the stage in front of us. The footsteps seemed to travel stage right. As I had locked the theater door after the last actor left, I am certain no one was in the building outside me, my son and my two friends.

Missy had a digital recorder in her car. She went to get it, and we had an impromptu EVP session.

I took notes. The date was April 17, 2011.

The session occurred upstairs in an audition and meeting room. We sat on the floor, in a circle, and placed the digital recorder in front of us. Drew turned it on and greeted Carl. He then asked that any spirit wishing to communicate knock once for yes and twice for no. Immediately, we heard a knock behind Missy.

When we replayed the EVP session, we all heard a clanking noise, metal clicks making a "dink, dink" noise. The pattern wasn't consistent. This is a noise we had not heard by ear in real time. The noise reminded Drew of people working on the railroad.

At one point, I asked Missy a question, after which one clear knock, indicating yes, was heard in real time, followed by a distinct, clear, loud, human-sounding whistle. The whistle was like the sound an obnoxious guy might make in hopes of gaining attention from a girl he finds attractive. The recorded whistle falls under the category of a Class A EVP, which means it is very clear and easy to make out with no vibrations present that make words fade away. Class A EVPs are understandable by all who listen.

While recording, Reese Christian's assessment of Carl being the equivalent of a ghost gone mad was brought up again, following which a growling sound occurred. I would classify the growl as a Class B EVP, meaning it can be heard but fades in and out.

During the EVP session, we turned the recorder off a couple of times due to trains passing behind the building. Just before turning off the recorder, Drew said, "There's our train." After his statement, when reviewing the recording, we heard a distinct Class A voice respond. It said, "No, it's not."

Two more, less distinct than the first, whistles were recorded.

At one point, Missy said, "If you are Carl, knock loud for us." Following her request, at playback, we heard a loud knock. The knock was not heard in real time.

The four of us remained seated during the entire EVP session. Still, we heard movement in the prop room. Drew asked if the presence was in the prop room. Missy's recorder captured one knock, meaning yes.

Drew asked the presence if it was happy. Two knocks occurred and were caught on the recorder, two signifying no.

Drew studied parapsychology under famed spirit chaser and author of more than ninety-five books Troy Taylor. He has also hosted or been interviewed on several paranormal-related films. In other words, he knows his stuff. One of the things I like most about Drew is that he mixes a healthy dose of skepticism with an open mind. He doesn't automatically jump to a "haunted" conclusion whenever someone whispers "ghost."

After the EVP session, Drew brought up a Kennesaw house investigation he was involved with. The house sat near railroad tracks. We talked about how trains are metal on metal, moving quickly along the tracks. The Kennesaw tracks run through Dalton and Tunnel Hill and beyond. While we discussed trains and energy exchange, a real-time single knock was heard coming from the prop room, seeming to concur with our line of discussion. A lot of towns close to railroad tracks, especially old ones, claim hauntings. We wondered

Upstairs, Dalton Little Theatre. When Drew Hester led an information investigation in search of Carl in 2011, one of the posters on the wall mysteriously slanted. *Photo by Robert Hartline.*

A Norfolk Southern Steam passing through Dalton, with the Gordon Street Bridge in the background. *Photo by Mike Woodruff.*

if there is a connection between the trains, the tracks and spirits that pull energy from them. The trains are creating a constant flow of energy, thereby creating a constant fluctuation in electromagnetic frequency. When you add or remove energy, you're changing the natural environment. Maybe it isn't so odd that Dalton has so many claims of hauntings. It is, after all, a railroad town. I'm not suggesting, necessarily, that the trains or tracks bring ghosts to Dalton but simply that the constant supply of energy feeds the ghosts Dalton already has, allowing them to be seen, heard and experienced more readily.

It's not surprising that Carl decided to stay on at the Old Firehouse, now theater, or that other spirits visit. If ghosts are energy, as believed, it makes sense that they need a consistent supply of energy to maintain. They don't eat or sleep; instead, they thrive by siphoning physical and emotional energy from the living. A firehouse is a high-energy supplier. So is a theater, where crowds gather and supply an abundance of emotional energy generated by surprised gasps, howls of laughter, tears of empathy and bursts of joy.

DLT offers regular top-notch live entertainment to North Georgia. Be sure to bookmark the DLT website, peruse upcoming productions and plan a trip to Carl's house soon.

CHAPTER SEVEN

UNDYING LOVE AND WAR

So many men left their hometowns to fight in a war that would rip our nation apart. So many women were left behind, their hearts torn in two. The lucky couples would be reunited after all the battles were fought and the dust on the blood-soaked fields had settled. Other lovers would not be granted such blessed fortune.

In January 1861, Robert Thomas "Tom" Cook was elected captain of the first group of Dalton men and boys to officially join the Confederacy. They called themselves the Dalton Guards. Tom was twenty-seven. Made up of some 110 volunteers in uniform, with 20 known pairs of brothers among them, the Guards were well versed in military tactics and were equipped with the best accouterments available.

The night before they left for service, the Guards gathered at the First Baptist Church of Dalton, where Judge Edward R. Harden delivered a stirring speech about their service to the cause. The next day, they boarded trains at the Western Atlantic Depot and set out for Camp McDonald in Big Shanty, now Kennesaw. They became Company B of Phillips Legion Infantry.

Tom, described as a "man of charming personality" and "a brave and gallant soldier" in the writings of Laura Kelly of Dalton, quickly proved himself a worthy leader. In July 1862, he was promoted to lieutenant colonel.

Meanwhile, back home one of Dalton society's belles waited for Tom.

Before leaving for war, Tom had won the heart of Jemmie Black, daughter of Dr. and Mrs. James A. Black of Dalton. Laura Kelly, who knew them both and who wrote extensively of the times, described Jemmie as "one of the loveliest ladies in the city, a typical brown-eyed southern girl with a gentle voice and amiable disposition." Tom asked Jemmie to marry him before setting out for war.

Dalton Ghost Tour actress Samantha Hall-Turner portraying Jemmie Black, who loved her Confederate soldier dearly. *Photo by Connie Hall-Scott.*

As Jemmie prepared for her wedding day, scheduled to take place on Christmas Day 1862, she was called to act as a bridesmaid for one of her friends. When the officiating minister asked her what she planned to do after the war, Jemmie informed him she had no higher aspiration than to become Mrs. Thomas Cook.

Just before the Battle of Fredericksburg, Tom commented to Sergeant A.W. Lynn that it would be "bad for a man to fight nearly through the war and then be killed." In less than two days, on December 13, 1862, Tom poured out his life's blood on the battlefield.

"No braver or truer man ever drew a sword in defense of his country," Sergeant Lynn said.

How tragically sad that when Jemmie's love was delivered back to her it would be in a pine box. Tom was laid to rest on what was meant to be their wedding day, Christmas 1862. He now lies next to his mother in the Hamilton Presbyterian Cemetery in Dalton. Though Jemmie would go on to marry another soldier after the war, move to Calhoun and live until 1885, it was said that her once vibrant brown eyes forever after reflected a subdued sadness.

The depot from which the Guards departed remains today. A nationally registered historic landmark, the Western & Atlantic Depot is one of the few train stations that survived General Sherman's March to the Sea during the war. The Depot also played a role in the Great Locomotive Chase of 1862.

Following careful restoration, the building retains its original architectural state and has served the community as a popular upscale restaurant since

1990. Patrons of the Dalton Depot & Trackside Tavern can opt to dine in the rear of the restaurant and watch passing trains from large glass windows. The depot stands in the center of Dalton, and the steel center marker from the original surveying of the city can be seen inside. It's located at 110 Depot Street in historic downtown Dalton.

One former bartender of the Depot isn't so sure Tom and Jemmie's story ended during the war.

"I have felt a presence there," he claims. "Sometimes I'd be behind the bar and feel a light touch on the back of my neck. I thought it was another employee goofing off the first few times it happened. But when I turned around no one would be close to me.

"There's a feeling that goes along with those types of experiences," he went on to say. "It's hard to explain. I guess you could say it's like a chill.

The delectable Dalton Depot Restaurant & Trackside Tavern today. When functioning as a train depot during the days of the Civil War, many soldiers left for war from this site. *Photo by Connie Hall-Scott.*

Old-timers might describe it as 'a possum running over your grave.' It's, like, an eeriness."

This paranormal witness told me about another employee at the Dalton Depot & Trackside Tavern who believed something otherworldly was afoot at the historic site.

"I dated a server who worked there for a while," he said. "One time, she was changing clothes in the bathroom after her shift. She said she took the clothes she was going to put on out of her bag, placed them on top of the bag and stripped her work clothes off. When she went to pick up the clothes that were supposed to be on her bag, they were gone. Gone!"

He paused to make sure I grasped the magnitude of what he was telling me before continuing with his story. And he glanced around to make sure no one else in the restaurant where we sat was listening to his account.

"She looked around and spotted them clear across the room in front of the bathroom door," he revealed. "The real kicker is she was alone in that bathroom."

Or so she thought.

"I wasn't there when it happened," the former bartender clarified. "I'm just telling you what she told me. I can say that she was shook up about the whole deal. As for who the ghosts are, I guess they could be a lot of different people. It makes sense to me that when a spirit visits a place he or she has a reason for being there. Something that makes them either want to revisit somewhere familiar or, maybe they want to go to the scene where something went bad wrong for them and try to relive it or change it."

After I shared Tom and Jemmie's heartbreaking story with the believer, he began to nod.

"Doesn't that make sense?" he asked. "It could be Tom looking for Jemmie or Jemmie looking for Tom. What's more tragic than planning to marry the person you love on Christmas and then burying them on that day instead? That scenario has all the makings of a haunting."

Tom, Jemmie or any number of souls who left from the Western & Atlantic Depot to defend a cause they deemed worth dying for or who were there to wave goodbye could have returned to the place where such intense emotions were felt and expressed. Trains routinely carried loved ones away in those days of war. Sometimes the trains brought love back, and sadly, sometimes they didn't. Perhaps, in this case, the question asked should not be who the ghost is but how many of them there are.

CHAPTER EIGHT

DISTURBANCES AT THE THOMAS A. BERRY HOUSE

In 2007, an anonymous letter was received by the Georgia Ghost Society, or GGS. The letter detailed disturbing supernatural events that were taking place at the Thomas A. Berry House. The letter writer asked GGS to come to Dalton to help rid the house of its squatting entities. Not only were residents of the home hearing sounds, such as footsteps, and feeling as if someone unseen was monitoring them, but they were also actually seeing full-on apparitions and experiencing uncharacteristically high levels of agitation.

Along with Bob Hunnicutt, Drew Hester is a GGS founder, and I was invited to accompany a team on the initial investigation, as was Atlanta psychic Reese Christian. Normally GGS does not share private investigation locations or results, but I have been granted permission from both GGS and Chuck Smith, a representative of the Thomas A. Berry House, to share parts of the following story. Other parts have been kept private.

The date was October 20, 2007, and the weirdness began before I even pulled into the driveway of 506 Hawthorne Street. I was talking to Drew by cellphone. He was already at the house.

"Everything okay?" I asked.

"Yeah," he said.

That's when a deep voice spoke up, saying, "Not really."

"What?" I asked Drew. "Did you just say, 'Not really'?"

"Huh?" he replied.

He hadn't, but I'm certain someone had. I didn't "maybe" hear the second response to my question. I heard it loud and clear. Drew hadn't. The voice would be heard again later on by digital recorder. While at haunted locations, it is not out of the norm for certain people—even groups of people—to see things, hear things or feel things that others in the same vicinity don't see, hear or feel.

Chuck Smith is the founder and director of the Carter Hope Center. Serving the community since 1998, Carter Hope is a nonprofit organization that provides a structured and safe living environment to individuals in need of a long-term residential program and spiritual, physical and emotional recovery from drug and alcohol addiction.

By the time I arrived, interviews with residents were taking place on the front porch while a train's whistle and a barking dog provided background noise. The Thomas A. Berry House was built in 1882. It currently serves as a halfway house. Some of the residents are volunteers, some are court mandated and others are spouse or Department of Family and Children Services mandated.

I listened as a counselor told of a thirty-four-year-old resident passing away in his sleep in 2003.

"It happened in Room 3," the counselor said. "He seemed to be in perfect health, but then his roommate woke up and found him dead. His drug of

The historic and haunted Thomas A. Berry House. *Photo by Connie Hall-Scott.*

choice had been alcohol, but he wasn't drinking and was having no problems at the time of his death. He worked every day and had no known health problems. It didn't seem right. No one really talked about his dying much until the problems started up."

A current resident called "Joe" spoke up. "I've seen ghosts here," he alleged. "Right on this front porch. It was a little girl. And I saw one in a room in the back of the house. I've heard them walking, like other people here have heard. I know what you're thinking too, but I wasn't on anything at the time. I'm clean now."

"The first ghost I saw was in here," another resident said, leading us to the living room. "It happened about two and a half years ago. I was walking from my room to the kitchen when I saw an old man. He was standing right there in front of me. He didn't look into my face, so we weren't eyeball to eyeball. He was misty looking. He looked like he was about to walk off, but he faded away. He had no emotion, no expression."

The ghost, the eyewitness recounted, appeared to be in his seventies. He wore a white shirt, had gray hair and was around five feet, eleven inches. His appearance seemed to place him in the 1940s or 1950s.

"I never saw him again," the witness said. "But it did scare me. It scared me good. I didn't believe in that kind of thing until I saw that man."

At that time, Chuck Smith told us the home once served as a personal care facility for the elderly, implying that the apparition in question might have been from that era.

"At first, I thought this was all a hoax," Chuck admitted. "I'm not so sure anymore."

Before the time of GGPS's Thomas A. Berry House investigation, Chuck's dog had begun barking at things unseen and behaving "differently."

A forty-eight-year-old resident told of seeing a little girl out of the corner of his eye. "She seemed to be about eight or nine years old," he shared. "I was sitting on the porch, and she came skipping by. She seemed happy but not of this time. It wasn't scary; it was just weird. She went on around the corner. I can't sleep much, so I'm out here a lot at night. That's when I saw her."

"A lot of people have died here," a resident called "Chris" said. "Someone died in Joe's room, Room 1."

"A guy named Harold died in the office when he was eighty-two or eighty-three," Joe piped in. "Might have been old age."

"A lot of people say an old man that used to live in this house a long time ago used to beat the crap out of his wife here," Chris said. "A lady who works here told me about it. What kind of energy do you think that sort of thing leaves behind?"

"Another guy who passed through here killed his old lady," Joe said. "They were separated and he walked right in her workplace and shot her three times in the head with a pistol. Talk about bad energy!"

Resident Leonardo, age twenty-one, saw a shadow in the form of a person pass in the computer room. He said he didn't feel threatened or scared, but goose bumps rose on his arms while the hair along the back of his neck stood up.

While the interviews continued, I wandered up to the attic to where three GGS team members had just finished an EVP session. Captured digitally was wall scratching in patterns of three, knocking and growls.

Psychic Reese Christian said the agitator in the house was a man who "wasn't nice."

"He was in his late twenties or early thirties when he died," she channeled. "He knew this place when it was vacant. He killed three little girls, and he's holding one of them hostage here with him."

A sensitive GGS team member picked up on the spirit of three girls immediately upon entering the home. She and Reese were in different groups and did not share information until later on in the night. It's interesting how similar their accountings were. Also, Reese was unaware of the resident sightings of the little girl on the porch until later in the evening.

"I think his name was Jimmy," Reese said. "He died not long after murdering the last girl. I think her name began with the letter *E*. The bad man died in a motorcycle accident. He was able to latch on to the earthbound spirit of his last victim before she moved on. He's very threatened by Bob [Hunnicutt, GGS founder]. In life, he was a small, scrawny punk who was knocked around. He took his aggression out on young girls. He and his last victim need to be crossed over. She wants to, but he won't allow it."

The name "Jimmy" was also picked up during an EVP session downstairs in one of the residents' rooms. Reese was not part of that group.

The sensitive GGS team member, who did not give permission to release her name, had a vision of a wooded area where Jimmy disposed of the little girls' bodies. She said they are still in shallow graves in a leaf-covered area and that the murders occurred in the late '80s or early '90s. She believes Jimmy found the girls within a thirty-minute drive from Dalton, perhaps northeast of Dalton.

"He had attacked other girls before he killed," Reese said. "The girls found him slightly attractive. He would brush their hair aside and tell them they were pretty. He took them off on his bike and hurt them. His hair was a little past his shoulders with a slight curl. He had a couple of tattoos. He was skinny, but his arms were muscular. He reminds me of a carney—he probably worked at carnivals occasionally."

"He had a bird tattoo on his arm," the sensitive team member said. "I feel his rage. I feel it strongly."

The usually passive team member had to leave the room because she said she had an overwhelming urge to badly harm Reese. The urge, she believed, came from Jimmy.

"He hid here at this house sometimes," Reese said before the spirit she called Jimmy had expended all his energy and faded to her.

Reese picked up on a couple of other spirits. One was a little boy who still plays with three pieces of a wooden train in front of a fireplace. The other was an older woman at the bay window who liked to rock in her rocking chair there.

No spirits were crossed over that night. GGS made plans to continue investigating the Thomas A. Berry House. Everyone agreed that not all the spirits there were benign.

The Thomas A. Berry House is a large, two-story, wood-framed Victorian Eclectic–style home with a sizeable wraparound porch and several types of wooden ornamentation. The front door hosts a large, oval-shaped beveled window surrounded by ornate trim. The rooms are asymmetrically arranged. Guests enter directly into the living room, or parlor, with the staircase and hall straight ahead. The dining room and kitchen are behind the living room. To the right of the living room and dining room are three bedrooms on the ground floor. The second floor houses three bedrooms and a bath. The interior walls and ceilings are plastered, the floors are wood and the molding and trim are wood. The wooden stairway has a cherry newel post and banister with wainscoting on the interior wall. There is a bay window in the living room and a rectangular, clear glass window surrounded by stained glass in the dining room. There are several coal-burning fireplaces with intact mantels, and many of the fireplaces retain their original decorative tile. One cast-iron, claw-foot bathtub dating from 1895 remains.

The house is located on an L-shaped lot with sloping terrain and lots of trees. It sits atop Fort Hill, overlooking downtown Dalton. Historic photographs exist that show the house once had a picket fence near the street.

The Thomas A. Berry House is one of a handful of Victorian-era homes that remain in an area that was once an affluent section of Dalton. It was built by the Reverend David P. Bass (1829–1895) for his daughter, Mary

Elizabeth, and given to her as a wedding present when she wed Thomas A. Berry in 1882. Reverend Bass was a prominent landowner and the second president of the Crown Cotton Mill, an important local textile industry.

One of the two children born to Elizabeth and Thomas A. Berry was married in the living room of the house in 1912. The ceremony took place in the parlor amid ferns, palms and an altar of greenery. After Elizabeth Berry's death in 1945, the house was sold out of the family. It has gone through a succession of owners and usages over the years.

"You can feel them here," resident Joe said of the ghosts. "They watch. I ain't ashamed to admit it; they scare me."

The Thomas A. Berry House is not open to the public.

CHAPTER NINE

THE GHOSTLY GOINGS-ON OF A LAW OFFICE

A favorite of ghost seekers in Dalton is the building that sits on the corner of King and Pentz Streets in historic downtown. It has housed a funeral parlor, bookkeepers, a bedspread company, clothing manufacturers, Morris Drugs, Owen Pharmacy and a sizeable number of attorneys over the years. It is also the scene of two deaths and, some believe, restless ghosts.

As I've stood across from the building, on the other side of King Street, telling ghost tour takers about the spirits that passed through when it was a funeral parlor in the previous century and about the cold spots, eerie feelings and unexplainable noises that have been reported, several guests have captured perfect images of larger-than-usual orbs around and above the windows on the top floor.

Well preserved, this brick structure with metal window frames and Gothic cornices was built in 1911 by Frank Manly Sr., an influential townsman who made his living from a machine company. Originally, it served as Carter Brothers' Funeral Home. The adjoining brick, one-story structure served as the body holding area, according to Leslie Waycaster, who owns the building and practices law there.

It stands to reason that the bodies of hanged men W.I. Umphrey and Doc Posey would have been among those passing through Carter Brothers' Funeral Home. Some believe souls yanked out of protesting bodies—such as Posey's—linger longer than more accepting souls. Posey made a protest at the Gordon Street Bridge where he was hanged. Perhaps he's making a stand at the last place in town where the shell of his body took up space before being loaded aboard a train to Atlanta.

Filmmaker, hand behind the pen of the *Daily Citizen-News* column the "Town Crier" and super creative guy Mark Hannah has warmer memories of Leslie's building. In 2009, he wrote in his column that when he was a kid growing up in Dalton and his dad used to ask, "You want to go get the best hot dogs in town?" he knew exactly where they were headed.

Leslie Waycaster, attorney and owner of the building that sits at the corner of King and Pentz Streets, beside a door that used to separate Carter Brothers' Funeral Home from the coffin showcase room. Cold spots are sometimes felt around this door. *Photo by Connie Hall-Scott.*

Mark wrote about the wonderful memories he has of going downtown to Owen Pharmacy, climbing up on a counter stool next to his dad and "wolfing down wienies, slaw dogs with ketchup and mustard and those big crinkle cut fries, not those skinny, potato-dust filled ones so many places have now. And a Coke with a paper elbow straw."

Prior to the construction of the building, a smaller structure stood for forty-seven years, having been erected in 1855 by the law firm of Hearns and Sterling. Roland Q. Hearns, one of the owners, died a few short weeks after the building was completed, but his partner, Colonel James R. Brown, a brother of the late governor Joseph E. Brown, practiced law there and, later, became judge of the Cherokee Circuit. Colonel Jesse A. Glenn purchased the building in 1858. Judge Leaner W. Crook of the Superior Court of the Cherokee Circuit worked from the building in 1859 but died during the Civil War.

It was during that war that the first known death occurred on site. The building was being used by the Federal authorities as a post office. George W. Anderson, telegraph operator, was a brave Confederate soldier

Above: The Waycaster Building today. Dalton Ghost Tour guests have taken interesting shots of this location over the years, many containing larger-than-usual orbs. *Photo by Angela Moss.*

Left: The Waycaster Building, up close. *Photo by Angela Moss.*

who served with the Forty-fifth Tennessee Regiment. According to Leslie Waycaster, a stray bullet hit Anderson in the lungs, leading to hemorrhages that killed him. An article in the *Dalton Argus* confirms this.

Prior to the war, Colonel F.M. Longley, Colonel John T. Ault and former Confederate Jesse Reed practiced law there. So did Colonel W.C. Glenn, who later moved to Atlanta and became one of the most famous lawyers in the South. Between 1865 and 1866, Mrs. McCarthy and Judge Rousseau ran a general merchandise store in the building. Additionally, H.C. Hamilton, a U.S. commissioner, and Brad Tatum, an internal revenue collector, made their headquarters.

Whether it's the ghost of the Civil War soldier hit by a stray bullet on site, Doc Posey or another reluctant customer of the former Carter Brothers' Funeral Home or one or more of the type-A personalities who practiced law or operated businesses from the structure, Leslie Waycaster's building seems to boast the occasional ghost. You know, it could just be some soul passing through that, like Mark Hannah, misses those really delicious hot dogs Owen Pharmacy used to serve up.

CHAPTER TEN

The Curious Case of Smith Treadwell's Tombstone

Wealthy landowner, state senator, wartime guard at the notorious Andersonville Prison—Smith Treadwell was a man who let no grass grow under his feet in life, but it wasn't until after he was dead and buried that he became, in his own way, famous. His remains lie six feet beneath the surface of Treadwell Cemetery, at Spring Place in Murray County, but whether or not his spirit is at rest is part of a mystery.

Shortly after his interment, something strange and unexplainable began happening to his tombstone, strange enough to have been written about in a *Ripley's Believe It or Not* column in the 1930s. The article gained national attention, and hundreds of sightseers from all over the country traveled to Smith's resting place to see for themselves the likeness of his face that is said to have taken form within the lines of the marble of his tombstone.

As many people witnessed Smith's face on his marker with their own eyes, the question is not if the phenomenon happened—it's why.

Smith was born in March 1818. In 1838, he was among the first to purchase land in the recently created Murray County. A few years later, he married Mary Mobley of neighboring Cross Plains (Dalton). The newlyweds took residence in Tunnel Hill, though Smith rode horseback to and from Spring Place, where he served as a county justice of the interior court. Together, Smith and Mary had seven children.

Before her death in 1851, Mary Treadwell asked her husband to "try to win" her sister Betsy's heart. Knowing her husband and children would be loved and taken care of by Betsy, Mary was able to leave this world in peace.

This page originally ran in *Ripley's Believe It or Not. Photo courtesy of WH Wolfe Associates Historical Publications.*

In November 1854, Betsy became the second Mrs. Smith Treadwell. This union produced eight more offspring.

Wisely, during the American Civil War, Smith moved his family to his Terrell County plantation so they would be out of harm's way while he was away at war. Although too old for active duty by this time, Smith was sent to guard Union prisoners in Andersonville, Georgia. Andersonville Prison, officially named Camp Sumter, was the largest Confederate military prison during the war. Almost thirteen thousand of the forty-five thousand prisoners died there due to starvation, malnutrition, diarrhea, disease, abuse and blunt weapon executions from guards.

In Robert H. Kellogg's book *Life and Death in Rebel Prisons*, a prisoner described his entry into Andersonville:

> *As we entered the place, a spectacle met our eyes that almost froze our blood with horror, and made our hearts fail within us. Before us were forms that had once been active and erect—stalwart men, now nothing but mere walking skeletons, covered with filth and vermin. Many of our men, in the heat and intensity of their feeling, exclaimed with earnestness, "Can this be hell?"* [and] *"God protect us!" and all thought that He alone could bring them out alive from so terrible a place. In the center of the whole was a swamp, occupying about three or four acres of the narrowed limits, and a part of this marshy place had been used by the prisoners as a sink, and excrement covered the ground, the scent arising from which was suffocating. The ground allotted to our 90 was near the edge of this plague-spot, and how we were to live through the warm summer weather in the midst of such fearful surroundings, was more than we cared to think of just then.*

Ghostly goings-on are regularly reported at and around the site of Andersonville Prison today. In this place where so many died horrific deaths, indistinct figures in the fog accompanied by sounds of screaming have been seen and heard. A stench coming from the area of the camp is often reported. Disembodied voices have also been reported.

It is unknown whether or not Smith Treadwell participated in the abuse of prisoners at Andersonville, a place prisoners referred to as "hell." It is unlikely that Smith could have walked away from such an experience unchanged and with it having no long-lasting effect on him.

After the war ended, Smith freed his slaves and moved into a two-story colonial home at Spring Place. He built and owned several wheat and corn water mills and several bridges in Murray County. In his twilight years, Smith moved several times, living in Tilton and Rome, Georgia, before returning to Spring Place in 1888. He expired this earthly realm on February 20, 1893.

A marble monument was placed at his grave. It wasn't long before visitors began to notice that the streaks in the marble resembled a man. Not just any man, but Smith Treadwell himself.

In his book *My Life and Travels*, former slave Levi Branham wrote, "I helped bury Mr. Treadwell but I did not help put the tomb to his grave. I was there a few days after his tomb was put up, but I never saw any sign of the picture which resembles a man. Within a year I noticed the picture...I think it resembles him very much. It seems to me that the picture becomes plainer every day."

In the months and years following the *Ripley's Believe It or Not* article, visitors flocked to Smith's grave. Family members and friends were bombarded with questions about Smith. People living in homes near the cemetery were visited by curiosity seekers at all hours. Rumors started to circulate about the man as well. Some said he was an evil man who murdered his wife. Others said he was a dishonest person and a bootlegger. Some called him a war criminal. His family and those who knew him vehemently denied the rumors.

The marker of Smith Treadwell's grave now. Notice the top portion is missing. *Photo by Robert Hartline.*

In 1951, the tombstone was stolen. Eventually, fishermen found the stone in Mill Creek near Dalton. By this time, Smith's family had grown tired of the phone calls, the unwanted visitors, the damaging publicity and the damage and vandalism taking place in the cemetery. They decided not to reerect the tombstone.

According to James Anderson, the great-great-grandson of Smith and Polly Treadwell, it was members of Smith's own family who "stole" the marker.

"I remember seeing a picture of the headstone in both *Ripley's Believe It or Not* and the Dalton paper," James told me. "Smith owned a mill on the river at the county line, and I was told he sold moonshine, for medicinal purposes. I was also told some of the kin who did not like the notoriety stole the top portion of the marker and threw it in the river."

The current location of the marker is unknown.

CHAPTER ELEVEN
CEMETERIES OF DISCONTENT

THE GRAVEYARD PHANTOM OF WESTBROOK ROAD

One day, my friend and local radio personality Larry Gibson, aka the Morning Mayor, called me up and said he had a book he thought I'd enjoy reading. I went by the North Georgia Radio Group office and was loaned a small book published in 1982 by Dr. Leonard Earl Patterson Jr. The sixty-one-page collection contains four stories. One story in particular, the "Graveyard Phantom," grabbed my attention.

The account interested me because I had wanted to know the location of this cemetery ever since running across a press release about it while working as the newsroom assistant at the *Daily Citizen-News* back in 1996. *Fate* magazine, a publication "always on the cutting-edge of the paranormal," had sent out a teaser to hook paranormal buffs who planned to attend that summer's Olympic games in Atlanta into buying their magazine that told where all the hot (or should I say cold?) spots are. One of those supernatural sites happened to be "an unnamed, almost forgotten cemetery just north of Dalton."

This cemetery, *Fate*'s marketing department claimed, housed graves dating back to the Civil War era, a glowing-eyed phantom and a subdivision with oodles of poltergeist activity. Jinkies! Let's go check it out, I suggested, calling one of the sisters I grew up watching Scooby Doo with. But I had not yet honed my investigative skills, and Angie had no idea where to look either. I asked around to no avail. At least, I asked as much as I dared.

Remember, these were the days before shows like *Ghost Adventures* made it (a little) less weird to openly ask about ghosts and orbs and ectoplasms. Time went by. I got married, had kids, got divorced and life rolled right along. I forgot about the cemetery until Larry Gibson called with the offering of Dr. Patterson's book.

The book told exactly where the cemetery is located. It's on Westbrook Road off Cleveland Highway. Once upon a time, it was an isolated and peaceful place. That's before bulldozers came ripping through the countryside in the 1960s to make room for the Meadow Park and Westbrook subdivisions. When you turn onto Westbrook Road, soon you'll see a smallish graveyard on the left. If you blink you might miss it. Oddly enough, the graves are laid out on the side of a large hill, random scatterings of tombstones somberly marking remains of predominantly black inhabitants. Many of the tombstones are broken, neglected and unreadable. A handful of the graves are sunken in, leaving clear outlines of where the earth was carved out in anticipation of impending residency.

It is believed that the first persons to be interred there, in an area that is now wooded and where a shallow brook once flowed, were pre– and post–Civil War slaves. Some perhaps stayed on after the war, as was customary, or were hired to work for the planter whose house was a few hundred yards away, on the opposite side of the hill.

I used to enjoy picking Marcelle White's brain on local history, legends and lore. I often visited her when she manned the Whitfield-Murray Historical Society. The woman knows her history. It's amazing what she can remember. Marcelle shared a lot of history with me over the years, some for stories I wrote for the newspaper and some I sought out when developing Dalton Ghost Tours. She was more reluctant on the legend and lore information, not putting stock in the paranormal, but she shared what she could, which I'm appreciative of. Regarding the cemetery in question, Marcelle believes the land was owned by William Hammond, who acquired hundreds of acres in the area and built a large house.

Mr. Hammond lived from 1792 to 1871, was a gentleman farmer and was husband to Lucy Carol Hammond, who was a descendant of Pocahontas. Records show the Hammonds had fourteen slaves in the year 1860. Marcelle told me there's another small cemetery on the former Hammond property, currently in someone's yard, but that the location is kept secret.

These days you can visit the old cemetery, walk under the giant oak that has stood since the origin of the site and feel the history that those buried there lived. But if you do, especially late at night, you

A view from the unnamed cemetery off Cleveland Highway, home of the Graveyard Phantom. Houses from nearby subdivisions reported paranormal activity in the 1970s and 1980s. *Photo by Angela Moss.*

could cross paths with a frightening specter that Dr. Patterson dubbed the Graveyard Phantom.

The phantom is said to look like a man of medium height and slight build, with a slow, deliberate, stiff-legged gait. He wears a jacket-like hooded garment and generally keeps his hands in his pockets, except when he raises an arm straight into the air in some bizarre gesture. Those who have seen him say he has a grisly, lifeless face that is thin, bony and white. His eyes are fiery, like two hot coals blazing from their dark sockets. He likes to glare but doesn't speak.

"Few of us would believe such a frightful creature could really exist, without having seen him," Dr. Patterson wrote. "But, those who have seen him have upheld the phantom's existence for years."

Dr. Patterson called one such person "Ann Powell," though I don't believe that to be her real name based on the disclaimer in the foreword of the book. Still, I'll stick with it. Ann and her family lived under a half mile from the old cemetery in 1971. One evening while washing dishes at her kitchen sink, she spotted a figure under a tree in her backyard through the window. She turned off the kitchen light and returned to the window for a better look. Frozen in shock, she saw the phantom glaring at her from beneath his dark hood.

"The minutes seemed like hours," Ann told Dr. Patterson.

She felt threatened. After making sure all her home's doors and windows were secure, she returned to the window to find the phantom gone. She would never see him again, but she swore she would not forget him. She was never sure whether or not the death of her grandmother a few weeks later was a mere coincidence. The sighting occurred in the month of March.

One year later, in March 1972, Ann's neighbor—who Dr. Patterson called "Mary Brewer"—was working late at her restaurant in Dalton. She had no prior knowledge of Ann's experience when she received a chilling phone call at 11:30 p.m. It was her eleven-year-old daughter, Donna.

Donna was hysterical. Mary couldn't make much sense of what Donna was trying to say, but she understood her daughter was in trouble. A second voice came online, Donna's friend Joan. Joan was fifteen, and the two girls, along with Donna's brother, were home alone.

Clearly terrified, Joan asked Mary to return to the house immediately. "Something" was outside, the girl insisted. As fast as she could, Mary locked up her restaurant and raced home, sickened by the fear she'd heard in the girls' voices.

As Mary sped down Westbrook Road her headlights illuminated what appeared to be her son. By that time, it was midnight, and she was none too happy to see her child out on the street. She stopped her car beside the figure, leaned across the seat and opened the passenger-side door.

"Get in the car," she yelled as the figure turned, revealing a hideous face that would forever be preserved in the dark folds of Mary's mind. Frozen in terror, as Ann had been the year before, Mary watched the phantom stiffly cross the road and disappear into the dark woods that surround the cemetery.

Mary told Dr. Patterson she didn't believe in ghosts or monsters or things that go bump in the night. Yet she couldn't make sense of what she saw with her own eyes, try as she did. It couldn't have been human, she told him.

Once the phantom was out of sight, Mary snapped back and sped home. All the lights in and around her house were on. Nothing seemed out of place save a lone basketball her son had forgotten to put away. Donna and Joan quickly opened the door and ushered Mary inside. The door was relocked, and Mary rushed in to find her son safely asleep in his bed. Relieved that everyone seemed okay, her full attention was given to Donna and Joan.

The girls told her about how they had been listening to music in Donna's bedroom and playing the board game Clue when they heard a loud car outside that sounded like Joan's boyfriend's loud muffler. Looking out the window, the two of them saw that it wasn't Joan's boyfriend. The car making the noise was dark, and it moved very slowly, as if the inhabitants were looking for something. It passed by the house a couple more times, again slowly, seeming to patrol the area. Curious, the girls went outside and stood in the carport. As the car rode off, not to return, Donna spied a dark hooded figure standing beside the road by some garbage cans.

Still disappointed that the car had not belonged to her boyfriend, Joan told her friend it was only Donna's "dumb brother" trying to scare them.

A feeling in the pit of her stomach told Donna it wasn't thirteen-year-old Billy.

When the figure began to hobble away, Joan yelled at it and began to walk after it, mocking its stiff gait. Swallowing down her initial fear, Donna followed. They teased and taunted until the figure stopped, raised its right arm straight into the air and froze for a prolonged moment before returning its hand back to its pocket. Donna, a few feet behind the figure, told Dr. Patterson that a chilling fear swept over her at that moment. Still, she reached out to touch it to see if it was just her brother.

As the figure turned toward the girls, they saw its hideous plaster-like face and burning eyes. Just like Ann a year before them and like Mary would soon become, Donna and Joan found themselves frozen by terror, entranced, seemingly paralyzed. After a few tries, Joan was able to scream. The shrill cut into what seemed like frozen time and propelled the girls to run.

Also like Ann had done, Donna and Joan ran around the house locking the doors and windows. Then they called Mary. Years would pass before Mary shared with Donna her own experience with the phantom.

Two weeks after Mary and the girls saw the phantom, Donna had a serious bicycle accident and had to undergo surgery. Exactly one year later, in March 1973, Mary's husband and Donna's father died. Mary always questioned whether or not those incidents were coincidence.

Also in 1972, a family in a home less than one hundred yards from the old cemetery reported unexplainable, frightening activity. The radio would come on by itself. The television changed channels on its own. Lights flickered. Objects moved. The disturbances got so bad that the family ended up moving and selling the house.

About five years ago, my friend Samantha Foster told me she had friends who lived in one of the subdivisions next to the old cemetery who claimed to have bizarre electrical disturbances in their home. Light bulbs regularly blew, and strange noises often woke them at night. They could never figure it out.

It is unknown to me whether or not anyone has encountered the phantom since 1972. Maybe you can find out on your own if ever you find yourself driving down Westbrook Road some dark night, especially if the month is March.

West Hill Cemetery's History and Haunts

If the historic Wink Theatre can be likened to a small-town version of Atlanta's Fox Theatre, then Dalton's West Hill Cemetery is comparable to our state capital's Oakland Cemetery. Both resting places are filled with souls from all walks of life, and both are the subjects of frightening tales of ghostly shenanigans. You can read about Oakland's famous haunts in Reese Christian's *Ghosts of Atlanta: Phantoms of the Phoenix City*, but you can explore West Hill's haunts with me right now.

On the national register, West Hill Cemetery takes up approximately thirty-nine acres. Roads circle and web out from the oldest part of the cemetery, the high grounds. Cedars, pines and hardwoods provide heavy cover for a host of Dalton's dearly departed. A Georgia Historical Society marker and a reproduced Civil War cannon greet visitors at West Hill's main entrance at the corner of Cuyler and Ridge Streets. The gates are replicas of the fence that surrounds the Confederate cemetery, located within West Hill Cemetery; both the gates and the fence were constructed locally by Manly Steel.

To the west of a Gothic-inspired chapel, built of stone around 1940, you'll find the Confederate cemetery. Simple granite headstones mark the 421 graves within, few of which bear names. The stones were supplied by the Bryan M. Thomas Chapter of the United Daughters of the Confederacy, a group still active today. A sizeable granite commemorative wall containing the names of interred Confederate soldiers and the four Union soldiers buried here is found at the entrance. Once you walk inside the gate, a grassy walkway will take you directly to a statue of the Lone Sentinel, a Confederate soldier who stands guard over the fallen soldiers.

According to local lore, the Lone Sentinel takes his job quite seriously. More than a few youngsters—and some adults—who have taken joy rides through West Hill at night swear when their car headlights hit the statue its head turns. I can't tell you how many times I've heard firsthand accounts of this alleged occurrence by adamant guests of my ghost tour over the years.

The Lone Sentinel was originally placed in Memorial Park at the intersection of Selvidge Street and Thornton Avenue in 1892 in recognition

This cannon sits at the main entrance of West Hill Cemetery. *Photo by Robert Hartline.*

Part of the old section at West Hill Cemetery. *Photo by Robert Hartline.*

of those who lost their lives in defense of the Confederacy. When Thornton Avenue was widened to five lanes in the 1970s, the Lone Sentinel was moved to its current and very fitting location.

West Hill Cemetery offers up a vast collection of grave marker types including obelisks and pedestals, die, case and cap, bedstead, raised top, plaques, ledgers, table tombs and box tombs. Some have unique shapes and etchings, from guitars to Uga, the mascot for the Georgia Bulldogs. Though most of the markers are traditional in style, there are a number of extraordinary stones, some of monumental scale, including two large obelisks and a sculptured angel on a pedestal. Mausoleums, large and small, too, can be found, most notably the marble walk-in Hardwick family mausoleum.

"You hear stories about the place," a now forty-something graduate of Dalton High School told me. He continued with one of his own:

> *I lived within walking distance of West Hill Cemetery growing up and once took a girl I wanted to get to know better to a particular mausoleum that I'd heard scary stories about. Someone told me that if you climb on top and knock, you'd get a knock back. I figured it*

West Hill's Confederate cemetery. *Photo by Connie Hall-Scott.*

One of West Hill Cemetery's angels. *Photo by Robert Hartline.*

The statue of a Rebel soldier stands guard over the 421 soldiers interred in the Confederate section of West Hill Cemetery. *Photo by Connie Hall-Scott.*

wouldn't happen and that if it did, the knock would be the product of an echo. At the time, it seemed to me a good way to get closer to the girl. She gets scared, she gets closer, that whole scenario. Timing was key for this operation. We went into the cemetery a little after midnight, climbed on top of the mausoleum, sat and talked. I set the scene up with stories I'd heard from people who said they had actually done the whole knocking thing. When the moment felt right I knocked, hoping for that echo. The echo didn't come, but at least a minute later, a very clear and strong knock coming from the inside of the mausoleum slammed the fear of God in me! I jumped off, twisted my ankle. Pretty sure my bravery didn't impress the girl that night.

Even now, the gentleman who shared the knocking mausoleum story with me believes his and his friend's experience falls under the category of paranormal, though as a mature adult, he said he never should have disrespected the inhabitants or the family of the inhabitants by climbing atop the mausoleum.

There are quite a few interesting tombstone inscriptions that offer a succinct glimpse of who lies beneath. "Be kind to one another," advises Daly Wallace's stone. "Be prepared," instructs the stone of Alton Dewberry. Charles Knorr's tombstone informs us that Knorr has "passed on to the next phase of existence," while Sallie Fain Wrinkle's epitaph describes her virtue by saying, "She extended charity, Do thou likewise." Mary T. Hyer-McKelvey's stone lets us know that "she and her babe sleep in the same grave." We are made aware from reading his marker that McAfee Bates Davis "lost his earthly life by car accident."

Members of a well-known Atlanta paranormal investigative team once explored West Hill Cemetery when in town to assist a family living in a historic home not far from the cemetery. I am told they ventured in at night.

"Things happened," a member of the team said. "Just walking around you can feel the energy of some earthbound spirits. There's a particular heaviness in the old section and at an old grave that belongs to a two-year-old little girl. I don't think it's the spirit of the little girl but more likely a spirit or spirits who feel territorial and wanted to discourage us from hanging around."

"I mostly felt peaceful there," added another team member. "It's a nice place to end up. Though I too believe there were spirits in visitation when we were at West Hill. When you've been around a lot of affected, or haunted, places you develop a kind of sixth sense. You are more aware of the things

Another of West Hill Cemetery's angels. *Photo by Connie Hall-Scott.*

that go along with disembodied spirits. I felt presences that night, for certain. I can't say who they were."

Though we can't pinpoint precisely which spirits have visited West Hill Cemetery, we can assume the spirits there are either residents hanging on to this life for some reason or visiting specters with ties to one or more of the interred.

You already know the sole recipient of Dalton's legal hanging—W.I. Umphrey—was delivered to a pauper's grave at West Hill Cemetery. The exact location is unknown. His grave is unmarked. J.C.H. Wink, who owned a chain of theaters in Georgia and Tennessee in addition to the Wink Theatre, lies at General Thomas Drive. There are politicians and

J.C.H. Wink rests at West Hill Cemetery. Mr. Wink is responsible for the beautiful art moderne theater that lights up West Crawford Street in historic downtown Dalton. *Photo by Connie Hall-Scott.*

decorated soldiers and generals and important businesspeople and artists and athletes and oodles of fascinating residents. For the sake of brevity, here are but a few:

ROBERT LOVEMAN, who lived from 1864 to 1923, can be found off Ridge Street. This eccentric and talented man was a poet and a songwriter. He authored the first Georgia state song, titled "Georgia," and the popular poem the "Rain Song." The last phrase of the poem, "It isn't raining rain to me, it's raining violets," was used in the first talking movie, *The Jazz Singer*.

DANIEL JOSEPH CAREY rests among fellow soldiers in the Civil War portion of West Hill Cemetery. Carey, who died in 1912, claims to have fired the first musket in the Civil War from Charleston, South Carolina, three months before action would take place at Fort Sumter. He was a cadet of The Citadel and was tasked with keeping vigil on Morris Island, an outpost overlooking Fort Sumter and Charleston Harbor. In the predawn hours of January 9, 1861, Carey saw an enemy ship attempting to reach Fort Sumter. After several hours of fire exchange, the ship retreated.

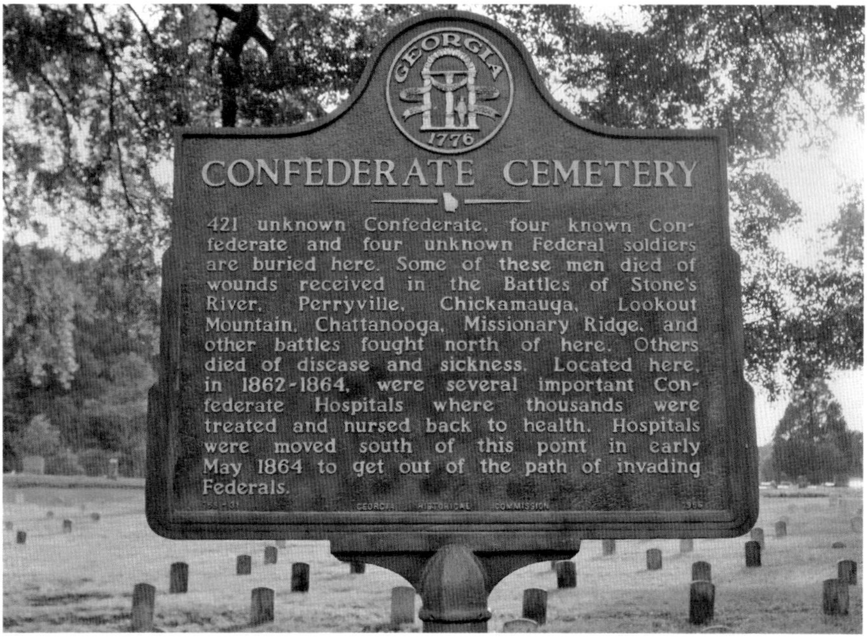

Confederate cemetery historic marker, West Hill Cemetery. *Photo by Angela Moss.*

CATHERINE EVANS WHITNER, 1880–1964, the shy second child of six in a farming family, began a thriving and profitable bedspread, robe and rug business that blossomed into the multibillion-dollar tufted carpet industry Dalton is famed for. I'm inspired by something she said when remembering her first bedspread. She stated, "My mother told me that I had started something I would never finish." But look what she did. She helped put Dalton on the proverbial map. By the time of her death, at age eighty-three, Catherine Whitner was said to have contributed more to Georgia's economic growth than any other woman in history. Many of us owe her a lot. She rests off Evans Whitener Drive.

HARRY LEON "SUITCASE" SIMPSON, 1925–1979, was one of the earliest African American baseball players in the American League.

DALE SINGLETON, 1955–1985, was a Hall of Fame road race champion motorcyclist.

ANTHONY JOHNSON SHOWALTER, 1858–1924, composed one of the most popular hymns of the twentieth century: "Leaning on the Everlasting Arms."

Whereas Atlanta's Oakland Cemetery holds the final resting place of Margaret Mitchell, brilliant author of *Gone with the Wind*, West Hill Cemetery holds Dalton's real-life version of Mitchell's character Rhett Butler. Hiram "Walter" Parker Bohannon, who lived from 1865 to 1959, was the son of a railroad man and the leader of a highly organized group of outlaws known as the "Bohannon Gang." They looted freight trains as they passed through Dalton in the 1890s. He considered himself a "profiteer," like Rhett Butler. He is said to have been handsome, charismatic and known throughout Dalton for his dapper manner, stylish dress and way with the ladies. Society women loved him. In August 1894, core members of the Bohannon Gang were captured. The sensationalized event was covered by the *New York Times*, and convictions for a number of Dalton merchants, businessmen and local political and railroad officials on charges of receiving stolen railroad freight resulted.

Dalton Little Theatre offers a Spirit Walk through West Hill Cemetery biannually, at which time the stories of selected cemetery residents are told by beautifully costumed actors. West Hill Cemetery is located near historic downtown Dalton between Emery, Cuyler and Ridge Streets. Visitors are welcome during daylight hours.

CHAPTER TWELVE
DALTON'S BELIEVE IT OR NOT

SKELETONS UNDERNEATH THE HOUSE

In May 1893, a Mr. Guider set out to dig a foundation for a new chimney hearth at his country home on Spring Place Road. His shovel soon hit what would turn out to be a well-preserved coffin, the top made of pine and the sides of poplar. Inside the coffin, Guider found a skeleton with every part intact, including twenty-three teeth. When he and a few enlisted men removed the coffin, they found another coffin…then another…and another…and another…and still another.

According to the *North Georgia Citizen*, six coffins containing the bodies of six men were removed and relocated. It is believed the dead men were members of Captain Bloodshaw's Missouri Battery, as the soldiers were camped on site in the spring of 1863 during an outbreak of smallpox.

Mr Guider, not wishing to live over a graveyard, ended up moving his house.

THE HAND AND THE BLOODY HATCHET

On the grounds of the Crown Cotton Mills is a man-made pool of water. In September 1929, a bloody new hatchet was found nearby. Caretakers drained the pool and found a horribly swollen and misshapen human hand. For three days, the community was horrified and confused. Then G.C.

This photo was taken at Crown Mill Gardens & Archives in the 1990s, before the pond was cleaned up. A bloody hatchet was found nearby during the Depression era, leading to the discovery of a severed hand. *Photo by Connie Hall-Scott.*

Paine, fresh from Atlanta, tried to collect insurance money on a fresh hand amputation. He claimed to have fallen down some steps, badly breaking his wrist. He said he "finished the job" with his own rusty pocketknife. When no one believed his saga, and when a formal investigation began, Paine hopped on a train headed back to Atlanta—without the insurance money and short a hand.

A Bag of Human Teeth and Al Capone

In 2000, a fire consumed the building that is Trevitt Hall, located on North Hamilton Street in downtown Dalton. The owner at the time was local businessman Dan McNeese. He once told me a chilling tale of what workers found during the cleanup following the fire.

As debris was shoveled away, something fell out of a fire-damaged wall. It was a bag full of human teeth.

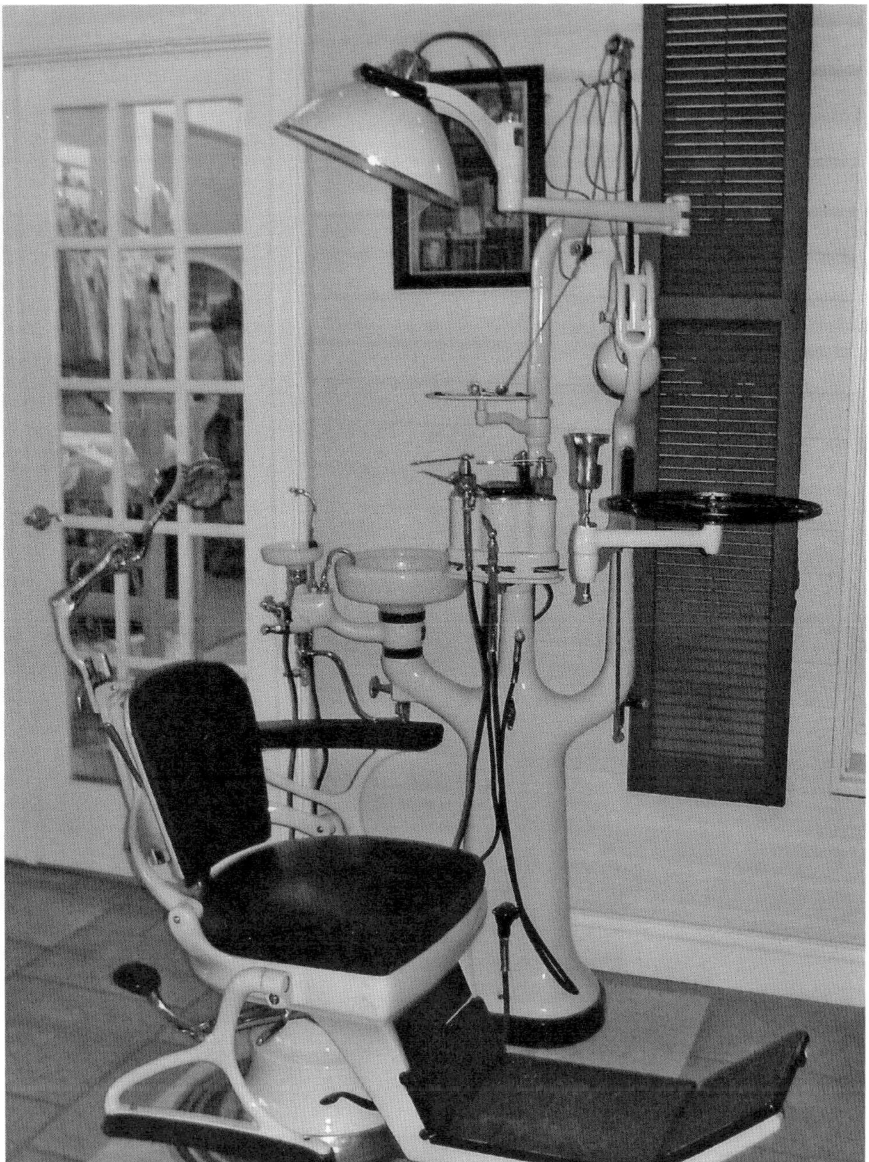

This dental chair belonged to Dr. Patterson, who once had an office upstairs at Trevitt Hall. Dr. Patterson was an alleged dentist to Al Capone when Capone was a guest of the Atlanta Penitentiary. *Photo by Connie Hall-Scott.*

Dan hadn't a clue why the teeth were there. He didn't know who put them there. A possible answer could come from the fact that a dentist, a Dr. Patterson, once practiced his trade in the building. Dentist or not, bagging up teeth and hiding them inside a wall is for sure an oddity. Whose teeth they are, how they got inside a wall and who put them there is a mystery.

I was interested to further learn that Dr. Patterson practiced dentistry on prison inmates at the Atlanta Penitentiary. One of his patients was the notorious gangster from Chicago, Al Capone.

He might have gotten away with murder, but he would not get away with shortchanging Uncle Sam. On May 4, 1932, after being charged with felony tax evasion, Al Capone was boarded onto a heavily guarded rail car on the Dixie Flyer. His destination: the U.S. Penitentiary in Atlanta. Dalton's newspaper reported that "half of Dalton" turned out

Photographer Leslie Jones took this photo of Al Capone en route to the Atlanta Penitentiary, going through Dalton. Capone is shown here with U.S. marshal H.C.W. Laubenheiner on the train. *Courtesy of Boston Public Library, Print Department.*

Dalton Ghost Tour actors Ron Chastain and Heather Foster-Ambrecht with Al Capone's 1939 Packard Limousine. Daltonian Charlie Hill owns Capone's car. *Photo by Connie Hall-Scott.*

to see Big Al pass through town on his way to the Pen. Capone would spend two years in Atlanta—where Dr. Patterson presumably worked on his teeth—before being transferred to Alcatraz in August 1934. Capone continued to control mafia interests from inside both prisons.

Several years back, I met Daltonian Charlie Hill. He's the owner of Hill's Used Cars on Glenwood Avenue. He is also the proud owner of Al Capone's beautiful 1939 Packard Limousine. Charlie told me a story about how Capone was agitated over a fella who owed him money. Capone and a few of his boys took the source of Capone's aggravation for a little ride in his limo and proceeded to beat the guy nearly to death with a baseball bat. Capone did the honors himself before opening the door of the car and dumping the poor man out on the side of the street.

If Charlie's car could talk, I'm sure we could learn a few more secrets about the man who terrorized Chicago.

THE LARGEST SNOWBALL FIGHT EVER

In March 1864, Confederate troops were camped in and around Dalton with five inches of snow on the ground. With little action going on in the area at the time, the men faced a new enemy: boredom. Soldiers being soldiers, someone decided to throw a snowball at someone else. A little snowball fight became a big snowball fight, and the next thing everyone knew, twenty thousand men were involved in an organized game of snowball throwing.

The Georgia and South Carolina troops gathered on one side of a small stream, and the Tennessee boys collected on the other. Battle lines were formed, drums were beat, bugles were blown, colors flew and officers mounted their horses. According to the January 22, 1887 edition of the *Quachita Telegraph*, every soldier started out with a knapsack of snowballs, and a small audience of ladies from Dalton and other nearby towns came out to watch the battle that would become known as the "largest snowball fight in history."

The Georgians started the attack by crossing the creek. The Tennessee boys, more used to snow and at an advantage, pelted the Georgians who were forced back across the water. When the Tennesseans followed, they took time to wet their snowballs to make the delivery more brutal. Some of the more overzealous men from each side began rolling their snowballs around rocks and other objects.

One soldier described the scene in Craig L. Symond's *Stonewall of the West: Patrick Cleburne and the Civil War* as a cluster of "pounding and thumping, and rolling over in the snow, and washing of faces and cramming of snow in mouths and in ears and the mixing up in great wriggling piles together."

The Georgia and South Carolina quarters were captured, with the Tennesseans looting "enemy" rations, tobacco, pipes and other spoils of victory. The Tennessee snow ballers were rewarded with rations of whiskey that night, and all the soldiers were treated to dinners of peaches and corn bread.

Though other snowball fights would take place that winter, the one springing from Dalton was by far the biggest and the rowdiest.

GENERAL SHERMAN'S CURSE

The bronze statue of General Joseph Johnston on West Crawford Street stands sentinel, the image of a man forever frozen in time, purposed to watch over Hamilton Street and historic downtown Dalton where his men camped in that cold winter of 1863 and 1864. Uncle Joe, as his troops affectionately called him, is given credit for having kept his one-time friend, from their days together at West Point, General William Sherman from burning Dalton on his infamous fiery March to the Sea.

I find it both sad and ironic that building after building has since burned to the ground, many within sight distance of Uncle Joe's statue.

Much of Dalton's business district burned in the Great Fire of 1911. That fire started in the building right in front of Uncle Joe in what was the original Hotel Dalton. It was the third fire to break out in the hotel within thirty days.

Along with Hotel Dalton, neighboring Dalton Opera House—where John Wilkes Booth's brother, Edwin, performed on a number of occasions—burned. Both John and Edwin were actors when the Civil War started, but the war would pit these brothers against each other with Edwin supporting the Northern cause and John supporting the Confederacy. As every good history student knows, John went on to assassinate Abraham Lincoln in April 1865 while the president watched a play at Ford's Theatre in Washington, D.C. Dalton Opera House was never rebuilt.

The bronze statue of General Joseph Johnston sits at the end of West Crawford Street, overlooking Hamilton Street. *Photo by Caleb Krout.*

The predecessor to the Old Fire Hall on Pentz Street was lost to the blazes that swept through the heart of Dalton in 1911.

Trevitt Hall, located at 111 North Hamilton Street, one street over from Uncle Joe, fell victim to flames in 2000. I remind you of the bag of teeth found during cleanup. The original structure was built in 1871 to serve as a center for community

Historic Trevitt Hall, Hamilton Street. Smoke smudges from a fire can be seen on the upper portion of the building. *Photo by Robert Hartline.*

The statue of General Joseph Johnston overlooks the Landmark Building. *Photo by Robert Hartline.*

activities. It opened on July 4 with a Hop Dance. Fire destroyed the building's interior, but the façade was preserved. Now beautifully renovated, Trevitt Hall once again functions as a place for community events.

Peacock Alley, the historic building that once held Fraker's Hardware, was lost to fire in October 2011, just one year after Hurt's Cleaners went up in smoke. Hurt's dry-cleaning business served the community from King Street in downtown for ninety-one years but moved out of the historic district after the fire.

The wooden deck from which Dalton Ghost Tours begin, directly across from the Wink Theatre, is the site of a small building that was claimed by fire in the mid-1900s.

Likely, the fires are mere coincidence. Or maybe they are the paranormal product of a long-ago wish made by a one-time enemy.

Uncle Joe died from a cold he caught while serving as an honorary pallbearer at General Sherman's funeral. The cold turned into pneumonia, and Uncle Joe was dead within a matter of weeks. But over 150 years after the Civil War, Daltonians and visitors to Dalton are reminded of his contributions to what proud Southerners once referred to as "the cause" whenever driving down Hamilton and Crawford Streets.

CHAPTER THIRTEEN

TERROR IN TUNNEL HILL

War at the best, is terrible, and this war of ours, in its magnitude and in its duration, is one of the most terrible.
—Abraham Lincoln

Disembodied screams reaching out from the woods in the dead of night, a headless phantom lurking around a Civil War–era train tunnel, mysterious ghost campfires, long-dead marching spirit soldiers and the smell of rotted human flesh—all things one might expect to read about in the latest Stephen King novel. According to some residents of Tunnel Hill, the same chilling references could be applied to their little corner of Whitfield County, especially when it comes to the fields and surrounding grounds where some of the bloodiest battles of American history were fought.

Tunnel Hill is a quiet community, with a population of 856, situated in the northwest portion of Whitfield County. Best known for its train tunnels and annual Civil War reenactments, the town is a popular stop for history buffs. More and more, it is also gaining attention with paranormal enthusiasts.

Ken Sumner of Woodstock, Georgia, claims to have experienced multiple encounters with ghosts in Tunnel Hill. Widely known in the area as a Civil War preservationist and reenactor, Sumner became interested in the Western & Atlantic tunnel in 1992.

Desolate and bordering on decay, the 1,477-foot railroad tunnel was in danger of destruction when Sumner and others decided to save it. Rumors of a ghostly presence in the abandoned tunnel have circulated for as long

Civil War reenactor and Tunnel Hill paranormal witness Kenneth Sumner. *Photo by Doug Smith, from the collection of the late Kenneth and Barbara Holcomb.*

as most can remember. It was during early preservation efforts that Sumner experienced his first peculiar encounter.

While approaching the tunnel with a handful of others, Sumner became mesmerized by a shape taking form out of the fog.

"As we drew closer," Sumner said, "it became obvious that the shape was the distinct outline of a human male standing just inside the tunnel mouth."

Intrigued, the group walked toward the figure, only to see it dissolve. Because of the fighting that occurred around the tunnel during the War Between the States, Sumner believes the presence witnessed by his group was likely the ghost of a long-dead soldier.

Another possible explanation was provided by Timmy Howe of Tunnel Hill. Howe remembers when his Boy Scout troop helped direct traffic at the annual Civil War reenactment in the early 2000s. He recalled a reenactor telling him about a circus train that passed through the tunnel once upon a time.

As Howe heard it, one of the circus workers—reputedly a clown—rode atop the train. A passenger riding inside the train attempted to alert the worker of the approaching tunnel, but the warning went unheard under the noise of the moving train. At the last moment, the clown looked up just in time to glimpse his fate. According to the legend, he was decapitated and now spends his afterlife looking for his head around the entrance and just inside of the tunnel.

"I don't believe in ghosts and stuff but I still wouldn't go through that tunnel by myself," Howe stated.

According to an article that ran in the March 30, 1916 edition of the *Daily Citizen-News*, showman Walter Lewis, employed by the Con T. Kennedy shows, had indeed fallen asleep on top of a rail cart while passing through Tunnel Hill en route to Rome, Georgia. When the train entered the tunnel, Lewis was suddenly aroused and sat up, his head striking the top of the tunnel. Lewis was found in a semiconscious condition by a companion and was taken to a nearby hospital. His scalp was almost stripped from his head, and his injuries were critical.

It isn't terribly surprising that a ghost or two would be attached to the tunnel, whether soldier, clown or otherwise. It is, after all, the oldest railroad tunnel in the South and the scene of the Great Locomotive Chase. It is also the reason for the formation of the town itself.

Construction of what would become the first tunnel through the Appalachian Mountains began in 1848 in the area then known as Doe Run. It took a lot of workers to make the tunnel a reality, and those workers needed food, clothing, shelter and entertainment. Their needs were met by people who came, took root and built homes and businesses.

Burrowing through rock is a rough and dangerous business. Death called on some. Several Irish laborers, tasked with laying the tunnel's brick lining, left the site in coffins. If you stand in the mouth of the tunnel and listen really closely, you might hear echoes of the Irishmen's songs bouncing off the walls with brickwork done in Irish patterns. The tunnel was completed on Halloween 1849. On May 9, 1850, the first Western & Atlantic train passed through the tunnel and the new town, Tunnel Hill, became one of the railway's major hubs.

Mystery has surrounded Tunnel Hill's Western & Atlantic tunnel for over one hundred years. *Photo by Robert Hartline.*

Tunnel Hill's W&A tunnel is a favored subject of area art, as depicted here on the side of a building near the tunnel. *Photo by Connie Hall-Scott.*

The tunnel was used to transport the staples of war—weapons, supplies, food and men—during the War Between the States. Refugees fleeing both South and North passed through, as did local folks going about their business. Much coveted by both sides, the tunnel was ferociously fought over for two years. Many men fell during the skirmishes, and the spirits of some linger.

Eventually, heavy railroad traffic and larger train cars getting stuck in the tunnel led to the creation of a larger parallel tunnel. Use of the first tunnel ceased in 1928. For seventy years the tunnel was unused, unless you count the kids who snuck inside for thrills on dares. As the tunnel fell into a dangerous state of disrepair, it became evident that preservation efforts were needed. After a lengthy period of restoration and rehabilitation, the tunnel was opened to the public in 2000, just in time for its 150th anniversary.

Tours of the tunnel, both walking and by an eight-passenger golf cart, are available through the Tunnel Hill Heritage Center Museum. The museum is located at 215 Clisby Austin Road and can be visited online.

Within stone-throwing distance of the tunnel lies property donated to the city by the late Kenneth and Barbara Holcomb. This is ground on which grisly fighting once took place. Confederate general Patrick Cleburne and his soldiers camped out there from 1863 to 1864 during one of the coldest winters on record for the area.

Conditions were harsh, and soldiers suffered. There were few blankets and not much to eat. Clad in battered clothes, some soldiers didn't even have shoes left on their feet. Five to seven battles occurred, with 277 Yankees killed in one battle alone.

"There continues to be no truth to the rumors that this field is haunted," Ken Sumner, acting as captain of the Thirty-fifth Tennessee Infantry Regiment on reenactment weekends, used to tell newcomers. He hasn't repeated those words in a long time.

"The battlefield is definitely haunted," he now claims without hesitation or shame. "Peculiar experiences began happening to me in 1993 and have continued since with varying degrees of intensity."

Once, when Sumner and a group of fellow reenactors set out to clear a wooded area for campsites, Sumner was overwhelmed by a sickening odor.

"It's like a death stench, the smell of rotted human flesh," he said. "On the first occasion I was affronted with it, I was the only one to smell it. None of the other men did, even though they were only a few feet away from me."

Since that time, many others have smelled it, sometimes as many as five or six at a time.

Hundreds of men and boys sacrificed their lives on this Tunnel Hill battlefield in one of the Civil War's bloodiest battles. *Photo by Robert Hartline.*

Sumner also tells of ghost campfires that materialize. On one particular occasion, he and another fellow went to investigate.

"When we got about seventy-five feet away, we saw a set of legs in uniform pants behind the fire. A set of hands reached out to the warmth of the fire. Then we saw another set of legs. As we approached the fire, the legs and the fire disappeared without a trace. After we retreated, the fire reappeared," Sumner shared.

That night the fire lasted two and a half hours, though the materialization of the soldiers spanned only a few minutes.

"It was a cold December night," Sumner said. "Most of the sightings I've experienced happen in the coldest part of winter."

Once, Sumner said, he saw a Confederate ghost soldier walking behind his tent.

"It was a particularly windy night. Every so often, the wind would just stop. It would get dead still. That's when I could hear the footsteps. It got a little scary that night."

Sumner believes the ghost he heard and saw that night was that of a camp guard because it performed the duties of a guard.

"I've seen soldier ghosts walk around the perimeter of the camp in spring, around a big fog that arises up that time of year on the battlefield. It's a circular type of fog that surrounds the [reenactment] camp. They just walk around the edge of the fog like they are securing their posts," he said.

The ghosts have gotten so active in one area of the battlefield that some reenactors refuse to go there. It has been said that these ghosts bang pans belonging to campers together and thrust logs against trees. Sometimes, they even manifest. One time, a group of people witnessed a ghost lantern floating across the field, and more than a few campers have reported hearing strange, inhuman screams coming from the woods late at night.

Those who have seen the ghosts commonly describe them as dark figures in human form.

During the weekend of the reenactment, participants dress in either Union or Confederate attire. The historically accurate, detailed uniforms appear authentic. When camping on site in full regalia, some say it feels as if they have been tossed back in time. It's not always easy to distinguish reality from supernatural once the stage is set and unexplained events begin to occur.

For example, on one night, a Confederate soldier walked out of the fog that is so common on the field. A man who saw him thought the soldier was a fellow reenactor, until the soldier disappeared before his eyes.

This photo was taken during an annual Tunnel Hill Civil War reenactment. *Photo by Doug Smith, from the collection of the late Kenneth and Barbara Holcomb.*

Tunnel Hill battle reenactment. *Photo by Doug Smith, from the collection of the late Kenneth and Barbara Holcomb.*

On another occasion, a group saw a Union soldier lying beside the road at the campsite. His head rested on a pack. He appeared to be sleeping. The group took care in walking past him, not wishing to wake him, only to look back to find the soldier wasn't there at all.

"Out here, your imagination can get away with you," Sumner admitted. "But when groups of people see the same things, it's pretty clear something is going on. These ghosts want to remind us, 'Hey, we suffered here.' If you are sincere, they pretty much leave you alone. If not, they may try to run you off. I have seen people run out of the woods screaming."

Sumner believes the ghosts just want visitors to remember the magnitude of what took place in Tunnel Hill and in our once war-torn nation. He believes they want their lives and sacrifices to be remembered, whether they fought for the North or for the South. Ken Sumner will continue to camp the battlefields of Tunnel Hill. He expects to experience more paranormal activity, especially when it's cold.

Situated between the W&A tunnel and the former battlefield is a well-maintained, two-story brick antebellum home, built in 1848 by Clisby Austin. Like the W&A tunnel and the battlefield, this dwelling played an important role in the War Between the States. And like them also, the Clisby Austin House, as it is commonly called, was left with a legacy forever linking it to the past—a legacy and, it seems, ghosts.

As battle raged and the number of the injured rose in Chickamauga, the Clisby Austin House was converted to a hospital. While fighting in Chickamauga, Confederate officer John Bell Hood was severely wounded, requiring his right leg to be amputated four inches below his hip. Believing Hood would likely die en route, the doctor sent along the severed leg with its owner for burial.

Like many before him had and many after would, the doctor underestimated John Hood. He was not to die yet. Known for his bravery and aggression, often bordering on recklessness, Hood was barely into his thirties when he lost his leg. This was the second major hit his body had taken since his time at war.

According to writer Georgiana C. Kotarski, author of *Ghosts of the Southern Tennessee Valley*, Hood left Tunnel Hill and went to the home of Colonel Frank Little in the West Armurchee Valley to recover. But when word spread that the Yankees were coming for him, Hood was moved by the Confederacy back to Tunnel Hill under the cover of night. Twelve slaves, working in shifts of six at a time, were said to have carried him all the way back to the Clisby Austin House down a dark road while singing to him. Hood, under the opiate laudanum, happily sang along with them.

The Clisby Austin House of Tunnel Hill served as a Civil War hospital. General Hood stayed here, and General Sherman planned the last leg of his March to the Sea here. *Photo by Robert Hartline.*

Legend has it that on his second visit to the Clisby Austin House, Hood's thoughts bounced back and forth between two women.

The first brought him sorrow and regret, for she was his first love and was forever lost to him. Perhaps he called out her name—Anne—in fitful sleep as he dreamed of strolling the gardens of his Kentucky homestead, hand-in-hand with her.

Often referred to as "the belle of central Kentucky," legend says Anne Mitchell was a young beauty, both gentle and sweet. Though she had her pick of suitors, there was but one for her: John Bell Hood, her tall, blond and handsome neighbor.

As the story is told, while Hood was away at West Point, a wealthy man—whose last name was Anderson and whose first name history forgot—asked for Anne's hand in marriage. Though she protested, her family forced her agreement. Anne wrote a letter to Hood, promising to love him forever. Upon receiving the letter, Hood rushed home to Kentucky. He was able to get a message to Anne, telling her he would meet her in a couple of nights and they would elope. Anne's heart swelled with love and hope.

Mere minutes after Anne left to join her lover, a Mitchell family slave alerted the family. Anne's father and brothers quickly caught up to Anne and John, dragged her away and locked her in her room. As the story goes, she sat staring out her window at the Hoods' gardens. Months passed, vows were exchanged and Anne found herself married to Anderson. In spite of the wealth and attention showered on Anne by her new husband, she refused to leave the Mitchell home and sank into depression and moodiness.

Legend has it that after the birth of her son, Corwin Anderson, Anne uttered a curse "upon all who had any part in making me marry another when my heart will always belong to John Bell Hood." That very afternoon, the sky darkened, a thunderstorm formed and a lightning bolt struck the Mitchell home. Three people were killed under the collapsed roof: one of Anne's brothers who helped stop her elopement, the slave girl who alerted the family and Anne herself.

According to several websites, subsequent owners of the Hood home are said to have reported seeing Anne's ghost wandering the gardens.

If Anne took a part of Hood's heart with her when she died, he was certainly practical enough to know he didn't want to go through the rest of his life alone. By the time of his stay at the Clisby Austin House, Hood was thinking more and more of another female: Sally Buchanan Preston, a flirtatious South Carolina socialite he wanted to marry.

With Anne, Sally, a freshly amputated leg and war on his mind, John Hood was far from at rest during his time in Tunnel Hill.

"Some of us have seen a candle burning in the upstairs window at the Clisby Austin House," one reenactor claimed. "The woman who lived in the house during that time said that's impossible because she doesn't burn candles. I've seen the candle myself. I have also heard tell of noises inside the Clisby Austin. They say sometimes when you're downstairs, you can hear what sounds like walking upstairs, although no one is actually up there to be doing the walking. What's more, the walking sounds like a heavy footstep and a cane hitting the wood floor. Some people wonder if it's John Hood looking for that leg he lost."

Hood's leg was buried in an unmarked location outside the Clisby Austin House.

"There are several areas where it is rumored to be," Ken Sumner said. "It is possible that it's by a split rail fence behind the springhouse toward the creek. That was before Ken Holcomb had that area filled and leveled many years ago. If this is where the leg is, it's now a good twenty feet down."

Several websites devoted to sightings of Anne Mitchell's ghost suggest her curse affected the object of her love and devotion. History shows us his career, health and private affairs were subject to touches of disappointment and tragedy. He would never marry Sally Preston and was, in fact, embarrassed by her rejection of him. He would, after the war, marry Anna Marie Hennen in Louisiana. Together they had eleven children, including three pairs of twins. In 1879, just days following his wife and oldest child, John died of yellow fever, leaving ten orphans who were adopted by families in Louisiana, Mississippi, Georgia, Kentucky and New York. He is buried in the Hennen family tomb at Metairie Cemetery in New Orleans, minus that leg.

One story circulating claims the spirit of General Hood can't rest with his body in one state and his leg in another. Maybe for him, home is where the leg is, making the Clisby Austin home. It has been said that he still makes his way across the floors of the Clisby Austin House with a muffled thump and drag but that mostly, he just sits and rocks. For a long time, a rocking chair placed in Hood's old room creaked to a back-and-forth movement made by someone unseen. Whenever anyone moved the chair to another part of the room, it would slowly make its way back to the window and gently rock.

Another famous—or, if you're from the South, infamous—Civil War general stayed at the Clisby Austin House. The seizure of Tunnel Hill was the first Federal action in General William Sherman's campaign to Atlanta. The house served as Sherman's headquarters during the Battle of Dalton. It was from the home that he planned the last leg (no pun intended) of his devastating Atlanta campaign. Sherman was in residence from May 7 to May 13, 1864.

"That's a pretty serious thing that was planned inside that house," Tunnel Hill resident Tara Smith-Linville recently opined. "Oh, the negative energy created by the enemy making plans to attack from within! How many Southern men and women lost everything because of planning that went on inside that house?"

When you walk the fields, visit the tunnel or explore the Clisby Austin House with an open mind, you can feel the impression history left behind. Tunnel Hill is a place that once hosted fierce battle, massive bloodshed, sorrow, loss and all shades of human emotion. It really isn't so hard to believe that those hallowed grounds are inhabited or visited by spirits of noble men and boys who gave their all to a cause they so strongly believed in.

If you want to get a glimpse of what life was like during those four years of American history when North fought South, mark your calendar for the weekend after Labor Day. Watch die-hard reenactors re-create the Battle of Tunnel Hill on the very soil where the historic events took place, view demonstrations, hear storytelling and buy food and souvenirs. And be sure to pay close attention to the movement you see out of the corner of your eye. It might just be a ghost!

About the Author

Photo by Angela Moss.

Connie Hall-Scott is a freelance writer and content provider for a host of regional and national magazines, websites, newspapers, businesses and entertainers. She is the founder and operator of Dalton Ghost Tours, a ninety-minute walking exploration of North Georgia's legendary past and haunted present. Visit her on Facebook or at www.ConnieHallScott.com.

Visit us at
www.historypress.net

This title is also available as an e-book